Sundance Choice

A Brief Research Guide

THOMSON

™

WADSWORTH

Australia · Canada · Mexico · Singapore · Spain · United Kingdom · United States

Sundance Choice
A Brief Research Guide

Custom Editor:
Mark Connelly

Project Development Editor:
Lori Peetz-Gud

Marketing Coordinator:
Lindsay Annett

Production/Manufacturing Supervisor:
Donna M. Brown

Sr. Project Coordinator:
Tina Esby

Pre-Media Services Supervisor:
Dan Plofchan

Rights and Permissions Specialist:
Bob Kauser

Senior Prepress Specialists:
Deanna Dixon

Cover Design:
Krista Pierson

Cover Image:
© Ross Anania/Getty Images

For information about our products, contact us at:
Thomson Learning Academic Resource Center
(800) 423-0563

For permission to use material from this text or product, submit a request online at
http://www.thomsonrights.com.
Any additional questions about permissions can be submitted by email to
thomsonrights@thomson.com.

The Adaptable Courseware Program consists of products and additions to existing Wadsworth products that are produced from camera-ready copy. Peer review, class testing, and accuracy are primarily the responsibility of the author(s).

Student Edition: ISBN

Thomson Custom Solutions
5191 Natorp Boulevard
Mason, OH 45040
www.thomsoncustom.com

Thomson Higher Education
10 Davis Drive
Belmont, CA 94002-3098 USA

Asia (Including India):
Thomson Learning
60 Albert Street, #15-01
Albert Complex
Singapore 189969
Tel 65 336-6411
Fax 65 336-7411

Australia/New Zealand:
Thomson Learning Australia
102 Dodds Street
Southbank, Victoria 3006
Australia

Latin America:
Thomson Learning
Seneca 53
Colonia Polano
11560 Mexico, D.F., Mexico
Tel (525) 281-2906
Fax (525) 281-2656

Canada:
Thomson Nelson
1120 Birchmount Road
Toronto, Ontario
Canada M1K 5G4
Tel (416) 752-9100
Fax (416) 752-8102

UK/Europe/Middle East/Africa:
Thomson Learning
High Holborn House
50-51 Bedford Row
London, WC1R 4L$
United Kingdom
Tel 44 (020) 7067-2500
Fax 44 (020) 7067-2600

Spain (Includes Portugal):
Thomson Paraninfo
Calle Magallanes 25
28015 Madrid
España
Tel 34 (0)91 446-3350
Fax 34 (0)91 445-6218

The Sundance Choice Database

Flexible and valuable!

You select the readings ... we provide your customized collection! Without a doubt, **The Sundance Choice Database** is the best way to provide your students with the reading selections that you want to teach—complete with rhetoric and writing instruction—at an ultimate value.

Featuring hundreds of classic and contemporary essay selections—chosen by English instructors from across the country—our unique database gives you the freedom to select only the essays or topics that fit your course. Each essay is surrounded by pedagogy that gets writing students engaged with the reading, and inspires them to do some original writing of their own.

A customized selection of readings made just for you!
The new *TextChoice* online system (**www.textchoice.com**) is the easiest and most flexible way to build your custom reader. Build your customized reader online, and receive a free evaluation copy!

It's never been easier to give your students an affordable, made-to-order collection of essays that you've designed . . . this PREVIEW and sample chapter will show you how.

An outstanding collection of resources—including our Comp21 CD-ROM—can accompany your adoption. See 6–8 for details.

Turn the page! Your brief tour starts now...

www

Preview

The Sundance Database readings were chosen by English instructors across the country

Each and every reading within **The Sundance Choice Database** is there for a reason—instructors *use them* time and again to teach writing and rhetoric. In designing this database, we interviewed hundreds of respected instructors and requested their input. The result? This database includes only the best, most relevant readings for your students. A perfect balance of classics combined with new readings—most of which have never never before appeared in an anthology—are available for your selection. Additionally, the source for the core selections in the database is our own best-selling *The Sundance Reader,* **Fourth Edition.**

So flexible, so easy to use! Ordering a custom set of readings from **The Sundance Choice Database** gives you the flexibility to select readings, add additional chapters on rhetoric, or integrate additional media tools of your choosing.

MARTIN LUTHER KING, JR.

Martin Luther King, Jr., (1928–1968) was the most celebrated American civil rights leader of the twentieth century. As a young Baptist minister in Montgomery, Alabama, he led a boycott of the city's segregated bus system in 1955. Influenced by the philosophy of nonviolent civil disobedience advocated by Henry David Thoreau and Mohandas K. Gandhi, King led many protest marches over the next thirteen years. He won the Nobel Peace Prize in 1964 (the youngest man so honored) and was assassinated four years later during his involvement in a sanitation workers' strike in Memphis, Tennessee. King's birthday was made an American national holiday in 1984.

I Have a Dream

nted below was delivered in front of the Lincoln Memorial in
8, 1963. This was the crowning moment of a massive protest
red thousand people from across the United States. The im-
rage Congress to pass sweeping civil rights legislation (some-
ng year). King uses familiar patriotic language to maintain
not be complete until full racial equality is achieved. The rep-
"I have a dream," "Let freedom ring" gives the speech a rhetor-
t one of the most memorable moments in American oratory.

you today in what will go down in history as the
r freedom in the history of our nation.

a great American, in whose symbolic shadow we
Emancipation Proclamation. This momentous de-
con light of hope to millions of Negro slaves who
flames of withering injustice. It came as a joyous
g night of their captivity.

ars later, the Negro still is not free; one hundred
e Negro is still sadly crippled by the manacles of
ns of discrimination; one hundred years later, the
sland of poverty in the midst of a vast ocean of ma-
ndred years later, the Negro is still languishing in
society and finds himself in exile in his own land.
today to dramatize a shameful condition. In a sense
n's capital to cash a check. When the architects of

STEPHEN KING

Stephen King (1947–) is a phenomenally successful writer of horror fiction. His books have sold millions of copies, and several have been made into popular motion pictures. His novels include Carrie (1974), Salem's Lot (1974), The Shining (1977), Firestarter (1980), Cujo (1981), Christine (1983), and Misery (1988).

Why We Crave Horror Movies

CONTEXT: *Horror movies (and horror stories) are designed to produce an immediate and powerful sense of fear on the part of the audience. In real life, this is a very unpleasant feeling, which people will go to great lengths to avoid. In the following essay (originally published in the December 1981 issue of Playboy magazine), King explains why moviegoers crave the synthetic fear provided by horror films. His analogy of a roller coaster suggests that the thrill in questions involve the illusion of danger combined with the comfort of safety.*

1 I think that we're all mentally ill; those of us outside the asylums only hide it a little better—and maybe not all that much better, after all. We've all known people who talk to themselves, people who sometimes squinch

Outstanding selections

Just a few of the readings available to you in The Sundance Choice Database

Rhetoric
Critical Thinking and Prewriting ▪ The Writing Process ▪ Developing a Thesis ▪ Supporting a Thesis ▪ Improving Sentences and Paragraphs ▪ Improving Introductions and Conclusions ▪ Choosing the Right Words ▪ Conducting Research ▪ A Brief Guide to Documenting Sources ▪ Writing the Research Paper ▪ Using InfoTrac College Edition ▪ Understanding Grammar ▪ A Writer's Handbook

Modes
Mark Twain, *Reading the River* ▪ Gore Vidal, *Lincoln Up Close* ▪ E.M. Forster, *My Wood* ▪ Henry David Thoreau, *Where I Lived, and What I Lived For* ▪ Stephen Jay Gould, *Sex, Drugs, Disasters, and the Extinction of Dinosaurs* ▪ Alice Walker, *Beauty: When the Other Dancer Is the Self* ▪

Outstanding pedagogical tools and visual aids that draw students into each selection

Every reading in The **Sundance Choice Database** engages and inspires through pedagogical tools and features—soon, your students are sure to begin original writing of their own!

Unlike any other custom database, **The Sundance Choice Database** offers full coverage of rhetoric, presenting topics that will benefit beginning writers as well as topics more appropriate for experienced writers. Additionally, a **model student paper** is included in each theme or mode, to give your students an idea of comparable writing.

Evaluating Strategy

1. What tone is established in the first sentence? What does the use of the word *victim* indicate?
2. Rendón includes a quote from one of his articles. Is this an effective device?
3. *BLENDING THE MODES.* How does Rendón use narration, description, and comparison in developing "Kiss of Death"?

Appreciating Language

1. What does the term "kiss of death" mean to you? Do you associate it with the Bible or with Hollywood images of the Mafia?
2. Rendón uses several Spanish words without providing definitions in English. What does this suggest about his idea of the United States becoming "acculturized" to Mexican-American culture?
3. Rendón uses both "Mexican-American" and "Chicano." What definitions of these terms are you familiar with? Do "Latino" and "Hispanic" have different meanings and connotations?
   by "cautious Chicanos"?

ng Suggestions

of death" you have escaped in your own
omised your future by taking

STUDENT PAPER

No Deterrence

1   Does the death penalty deter anyone? One of the main arguments people use to support capital punishment is deterrence—the idea that seeing someone executed will make others think before committing a similar crime. In theory it might have that effect. If a gang member murdered a police officer or shot up a liquor store and killed six people, maybe executing him within a year of conviction might influence other gang members and younger people who admired him.

2   But today people spend years, sometimes decades, on death row before being executed. Stays and appeals delay executions to the point that any deterrent factor is lost. When a 38-year-old man is executed for a crime he committed when he was 25, who will be deterred? No doubt his gang no longer exists. The current generation of young criminals can't relate to him and don't see his fate connected to theirs. In addition, whatever shock and horror people felt by an outrageous crime has long worn off. Executing someone years after the crime becomes only an afterthought, a minor news item. Any deterrent power is long gone.

Within each theme or mode, two **images** are available for selection. Each visual within the image bank is accompanied by questions, writing assignments, and collaborative activities.

Responding to Images

Responding to Images

Sojourner Truth, *Ain't I a Woman?* ▪ Bruno Bettleheim, *The Holocaust* ▪ Nancy Gibbs, *When Is It Rape?* ▪ Michael Dorris, *Fetal Alcohol Syndrome* ▪ George Orwell, *A Hanging* ▪ Edward Koch, *Death and Justice: How Capital Punishment Affirms Life* ▪ Daniel Lashof, *Earth's Last Gasp?* ▪ Joycelyn Tomkin, *Hot Air* ▪ Anna Quindlen, *Horrors: Girls With Gavels! What A Difference a Day Makes. And If the Boys Stay Home— Well, There's a Lesson There, Too* ▪ Judith Viorst, *Bones Break, But Boys Endure* ▪ Ellen Goodman, *Girls Will Be Girls, Unfortunately*

Reflected in the **Database's themes**

Fourteen thematic categories are included in **The Sundance Choice Database** to help students identify with the readings. The latest issues are examined within the following themes:

- American Identity: Melting Pot or Mosaic?
- The War on Terrorism
- Medical Malpractice
- Reparations for Slavery
- Fatherhood
- Abortion: Roe vs. Wade at Thirty
- Islam and the West
- Capital Punishment
- Immigration
- Global Warming
- Public Schools
- America's Role in the Twenty-First Century
- Gender Identity: Raising Boys and Girls
- Welfare to Work

Themes that speak to students

Medical Malpractice

The health and life of my patients will be my first consideration.
–The Hippocratic Oath

The problem with medical malpractice is that it occurs far too often. It is the eighth leading cause of death in America, killing more people than AIDS, breast cancer, or automobile crashes.
–Leo Boyle

The villain, I believe, is our legal system, which has become a free-for-all, lacking the reliability and consistency that are essential to everyone, especially doctors and patients. Most victims of error get nothing, while others win lottery-like jury awards even when the doctor did nothing wrong.
–Philip K. Howard

I am sure I could have become a millionaire by suing my father's doctors and the hospital. . . . But I didn't. . . . [T]o sue someone for failing to be the god we wanted strikes me as wrong.
–Alden Blodget

OMFORT ALWAYS"

icians in the United States had only a fragmen-
icine. Few medical schools were affiliated with
not even accredited. Some medical schools did
ve a high school diploma. In a few states it was
l license in six months. Apprenticed to older
earned primarily by observation. There were
es, and little connection was made between
ped with dubious medicines and crude surgical
quently able to provide little more than emo-
at many conditions, physicians attempted only

The War on Terrorism

How can you defeat an enemy who thinks he's on a mission from God? How? A hundred days and one war later, we know the answer: B-52's, for starters.
–Charles Krauthammer

The instinct to retaliate with bombing is an anachronism. Fewer than twenty men had brought us to our national knees. . . . The government's answer was that we were good and love freedom and these people are bad and hate it. That vapid answer came from a national culture that has lost its talent for healthy guilt.
–Daniel C. Maguire

[W]e hit Saddam for one simple reason: because we could, and because he deserved it and because he was right in the heart of that world. And don't believe the nonsense that this has had no effect. Every neighboring government—and 98 percent of terrorism is about what governments let happen—got the message. If you talk to U.S. soldiers in Iraq they will tell you this is what the war was about.
–Thomas L. Friedman

Real wars are not metaphors. And real wars have a beginning and an end. . . . But the war that has been decreed by the Bush administration will never end. That is one sign that it is not a war, but, rather, a mandate for expanding the use of American power.
–Susan Sontag

On the morning of September 11, 2001, President Bush was visiting a school. Informed that two planes had just crashed into the World Trade Center, Andrew Card, the White House Chief of Staff, interrupted the ceremony and whispered to the President, "America is under attack."
But was America at war?

Complete with customized technology integration

No other publisher offers a custom database of this quality with technology integrated into each customized reader. When you adopt **The Sundance Choice Database,** you have the option of choosing from a menu of interactive technology tools—each of which will be carefully integrated into your customized reader.

Companion Website

See **http://sundance.wadsworth.com** for information on writing process papers.

E Reading: InfoTrac College Edition
http://www.infotrac-college.com

For Further Reading
E–Readings Online

Search for articles by author or title in InfoTrac College Edition after entering your user name and password.

Barbara Hemphill, *Who Are You?*
Specific steps can protect consumers against identity theft.

Lance Davis, *Cities Use Environmental Design to Combat Crime.*
Cities use three principles in designing public buildings to deter crime.

San Fernando Valley Business Journal, *The Interview Process—How to Select the "Right" Person*
Employers can improve their ability to locate and hire the best applicants by improving their interview techniques.

Mark Moring, *This is Not Your High School English Class*
Moring explains how improved time management and study skills can help college students cope.

Louise S. Durham, *Climate of Controversy: The Causes of Global Warming Are Still a Matter of Debate, but It's Worth Understanding How the Process Works*

Two interactive and easy-to-use technology tools that are FREE with your adoption and can be integrated in your own reader are:

■ **Comp21: Composition in the 21st Century:** The first CD-ROM designed to help students navigate today's new writing contexts and to incorporate new sources. The CD-ROM includes visual libraries, audio and video galleries, and collections of classic essays and speeches to add texture and depth to student projects. The CD-ROM is linked to each theme or mode in the **Database.**

■ **InfoTrac College Edition with InfoMarks™.** Each theme or mode in the Database ends with a list of further readings on **InfoTrac College Edition with InfoMarks™,** a fully searchable database offering more than 20 years worth of full-text articles. *See page 6 for a complete description of* **InfoTrac College Edition.**

Clearly integrated technology

Reliable, cutting-edge web resources

That make research easy for students

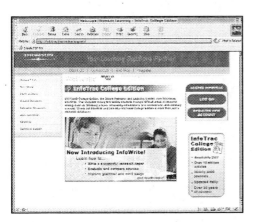

InfoTrac® College Edition with InfoMarks™

NOT SOLD SEPARATELY. This fully searchable database offers more than 20 years' worth of full-text articles (not abstracts) from almost 5,000 diverse sources, such as top academic journals, newsletters, and up-to-the-minute periodicals including *Time, Newsweek, Science, Forbes,* and *USA Today.* **NEW!** Your 4-month free subscription now includes instant access to virtual readers drawing from the vast **InfoTrac College Edition** library and hand-selected to work with your book. In addition, students have instant access to *InfoWrite,* which includes guides to writing research papers, grammar, "critical thinking" guidelines, and much more. Adopters and their students receive FREE unlimited access to **InfoTrac College Edition with InfoMarks** for four months. To take a quick tour of InfoTrac, visit **http://www.infotrac-college.com** and select the "User Demo." *(Journals subject to change. Certain restrictions may apply. For additional information, please consult your local Thomson representative.)*

Opposing Viewpoints Resource Center

0-534-12853-X

NOT SOLD SEPARATELY. This online center helps you expose your students to all sides of today's most compelling social and scientific issues, from genetic engineering to environmental policy, prejudice, abortion, health care reform, violence in the media, and much more. **The Opposing Viewpoints Resource Center** draws on Greenhaven Press's acclaimed social issues series, popular periodicals and newspapers, and core reference content from other Gale and Macmillan Reference USA sources. The result is a dynamic online library of current events topics—the facts as well as the arguments as articulated by the proponents and detractors of each position. Visit **http://www.gale.com/OpposingViewpoints.** *For college and university adopters only.*

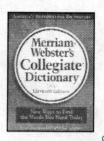

Table of Contents

Critical Thinking and Prewriting

*It is part of the business of the writer . . . to
examine attitudes, to go beneath
the surface, to tap the source.*
James Baldwin

Good writing is never "about" a topic—it has a purpose and makes a point. An essay about your summer vacation can be simply a list of places you visited and things you did, or it can focus on something deeper, something more significant, such as how visiting Mount Rushmore made you contemplate American values, how traveling together helped you appreciate your family, how spending a weekend in a cabin without electricity led you to discover how lost you feel without the Internet. A good paper shares more than facts and dates, first impressions, or immediate reactions. Good writing seeks to get beyond the obvious to explore ideas and events, to analyze people and ideas.

For example, if you decide to write an essay about your first apartment, your first thought might be to record every detail you can remember, trying to capture on paper what the apartment looked like:

On August 12, 2003, I moved into my first apartment. It was a flat on Newhall Street on the top floor of a hundred-year-old house. The living room was massive and had wood paneling and antique brass chandeliers. The dining room had a huge built-in buffet and china cabinets with glass doors I used as bookcases. The kitchen was L-shaped and narrow, but there was a pantry with lots of shelves. The battered refrigerator was old but spacious.

There were two big bedrooms. I planned to use the front bedroom for my study. The back bedroom was a bit smaller, but it had a great advantage. It was away from the street and shielded from the noise of traffic. In addition, there were awnings that blocked the morning sun so I could sleep late on weekends. The bedrooms did not have any closets. Instead there were large two-door wardrobes with built-in drawers. There was a spacious balcony off the front bedroom. It was covered by a redwood deck and had new patio furniture and an outdoor grill.

I had little money and had to get furniture from Goodwill and the Salvation Army. The floors were bare, but I covered them with old carpeting from my parents' house.

This approach will probably create an essay that lists physical details of minimal interest to anyone else. Before beginning to write, you might think about the topic and ask yourself some questions:

Why did I choose this topic?
Of all the possible subjects, why did you decide to write about your first apartment? What made you think of that rather than your first car, your last boss, a trip to New York, or a recent job interview? Clearly, something about that apartment made it significant. What did it represent to you? What events took place there that changed your life? Are your memories of this place happy or sad? Why?

What are the most significant details?
Instead of listing everything you can remember about your subject, select the most memorable details. Is the date you moved or the number of bedrooms really important?

How can I share my thoughts and feelings with readers?
Readers may not be interested in a room-by-room description of an apartment, but they may be able to identify with more universal experiences, thoughts, or emotions. How did you feel about moving? What change did it make in your life? What are the larger issues that other people can relate to?

What is the dominant impression I want to leave readers with?
Focusing on a single impression or message can help you select details. If you concentrate on describing your excitement about getting your first apartment, you can ignore irrelevant details such as dates, furnishings, and parking.

Considering these questions can help create an essay that has greater meaning for both you and your reader:

In August I moved into my first apartment, a great flat on Newhall Street. Although I could only afford to furnish it with battered items from Goodwill and the Salvation Army, I was excited. I was finally going to be on my own, free of my parents, my cramped room, my sisters' fighting, my brother's stereo. I spent two weeks cleaning, painting, and organizing the old flat into *my home.* I hung up posters of my favorite bands, stocked the kitchen with my favorite foods, and set the radio to my favorite stations. I was finally on my own, free at last.

But coming home from class, I was struck by the silence. Instead of hearing the drone of my brother's stereo, my sisters' laughing and fighting, I heard the hum of the refrigerator and the nervous tick-tick of an electric clock. I always hated that my mother watched soap operas but found myself turning the television on in the afternoon to hear the hated but familiar voices while I labored over algebra or ironed clothes.

On weekends I went home—not to raid the kitchen or borrow money. I had been adult. I had been responsible. I saved money over the summer and budgeted it carefully. I could easily afford my new apartment. I had hungered for a place of my own all through high school. But I never imagined what it would feel like to go to bed and to wake up in an empty house.

By thinking more deeply about a subject you can probe its depth, developing writing that does more than simply report facts and record observations.

Critical thinking involves moving beyond first impressions by carefully analyzing subjects, people, and ideas. Too often we rush to judgment, making instant assumptions based on what we think we know rather than what we can prove. We confuse opinions with facts, accept statistics without question, and let stereotypes color our evaluations. We allow what we "feel" to short-circuit how we think:

> Pete Wilson was a great quarterback—he'll make a great coach.
> Nancy's driving a BMW. Her new travel agency must be a success.
> Alabama improved reading scores 12% using this program; our schools should use it, too.
> Speedy Lube ruined my car. Two days after I went there for an oil change my transmission went out.

All these statements make a kind of sense at first glance. But further analysis will lead you to question their validity:

> Does a skilled quarterback necessarily know how to coach—how to inspire, manage, and teach other players, especially those on defense?

> Does Nancy even own the BMW she was seen driving? Did she get it as a gift, pay for it with existing savings, borrow it from a friend, or lease it at a low rate? Does the car really prove anything about the success or failure of her travel agency?

Alabama may have improved reading scores with a particular program, but does that really prove the program will work in Nevada or Minnesota? Could children in other states have low reading scores caused by other reasons than those in Alabama?

Did Speedy Lube ruin your transmission? They may have only changed the oil and never touched the transmission. Had you driven through a car wash the day before, could you just as easily blame them?

Errors like these are easy to make. Unless you develop critical thinking skills, you can be impressed by evidence that at first seems reliable and convincing.

AVOIDING ERRORS IN CRITICAL THINKING

Lapses in critical thinking are often called logical fallacies. In reading the works of others and developing your own ideas, try to avoid these common mistakes:

- **Hasty generalizations.** If your dorm room is robbed, a friend's car stolen from the Student Union parking lot, and a classmate's purse snatched on her way to class, you might assume that the campus is experiencing a crime wave. The evidence seems compelling because it is immediate and personal. But it does not prove there is an increase in campus crime. In fact, crime could be dropping and you and your friends could have the misfortune to fall into the declining group of victims. Only a comparative review of police and security reports would prove if crime is increasing. Resist jumping to conclusions.
- **Absolute statements.** Although it is important to convince readers by making strong assertions, avoid absolute claims that can be dismissed with a single exception. If you write "All professional athletes today are irresponsible," readers only need to think of a single exception to dismiss your argument. A qualified remark, however, is harder to disprove. The claim that "Many professional athletes today are irresponsible" acknowledges that exceptions exist.
- *Non sequitur* **(it does not follow).** Avoid making assertions based on irrelevant evidence: "Jill Klein won an Oscar for best actress last year— she'll be great on Broadway." Although an actor might succeed on film, she may lack the ability to perform on stage before a live audience. The skills and style suited for film acting do not always translate well to the theater.

- **Begging the question.** Do not assume what has to be proved: "These needless math classes should be dropped because no one uses algebra and geometry after they graduate." This statement makes an assertion, but it fails to prove that the courses are needless or that "no one" uses mathematics outside of academics.
- **False dilemma.** Do not offer or accept only two alternatives to a problem: "Either employees must take a wage cut, or the company will go bankrupt." This statement ignores other possible solutions such as raising prices, lowering production costs, or increasing sales.
- **False analogy.** Comparisons make very weak arguments: "Crack cocaine should be legalized since Prohibition did not work." Alcohol and crack cocaine are not similar substances. Alcohol has been consumed by humans for thousands of years. Crack cocaine has never been socially acceptable to most Americans.
- **Red herring.** Resist the temptation to dodge the real issue by drawing attention to something controversial: "How can you endorse the budget proposal of a member of Congress indicted for soliciting bribes?" Corruption charges alone do not invalidate a politician's policies.
- **Borrowed authority.** Avoid assuming that an expert in one field can be accepted as an authority in another: "Senator Goode claims Italy will win the World Cup." A respected senator may have no more insight into soccer than a cab driver or a hairdresser. Celebrity endorsements are common examples of borrowed authority.
- *Ad hominem* **(attacking the person).** Attack ideas, not the people who advocate them: "The only people who drive SUVs are spoiled, selfish baby boomers who don't care about the environment." The merits of the issue, not the personalities, have to be discussed to create a convincing argument.
- **Assuming past events will predict the future.** During the oil crisis of the 1970s, the price of oil soared from $10 to $40 a barrel. Alarmists predicted financial disaster, with Americans paying $50–$100 a barrel for oil to run cars and to fuel industry. But the dramatic price escalation was short lived. Price increases spurred exploration for new oil fields and launched conservation efforts. Soon the world was awash in surplus oil, and prices dropped to precrisis levels. *Past trends cannot be assumed to continue into the future.*
- **Ignoring alternative interpretations.** Even objective facts can be misleading. If reseach shows that reports of child abuse in your state have jumped 250 percent in the last ten years, does that mean that child abuse is on the rise? Or could those numbers reflect more rigorous reporting methods or an expanded definition of abuse so that previously unrecorded incidents are now counted?
- **"Filtering" data.** If you begin with a preconceived thesis, you may consciously or unconsciously select evidence that supports your view and omit

evidence that contradicts it. Good analysis is objective; it does not consist of simply collecting facts to support a previously held conviction.

- **Assuming that parts represent the whole.** Just because one or more patients respond favorably to a new drug does not mean that it will cure all people suffering from the same disease. In the extreme, because individual men and women die does not mean the human race will eventually become extinct.

- **Assuming the whole represents each part.** If 50 percent of students on campus receive financial aid, it does not mean you can assume that half the English majors receive aid. The student population in any given department may be greater or less than the college average.

- **Mistaking a time relationship for a cause (post hoc ergo propter hoc).** If your brakes fail after taking your car into the dealer for a tuneup, does that mean the mechanics are to blame? Can the president take credit for a drop in unemployment six months after signing a labor bill? Because events occur over time, it can be easy to assume an action that precedes another is a cause. The mechanics may have not touched your brakes, which were bound to wear out with or without a tuneup. A drop in unemployment could be caused by a decline in interest rates or an upsurge in exports and may have nothing to do with a labor bill. *Do not assume events were caused by preceding events.*

- **Mistaking an effect for a cause.** Early physicians saw fever as a cause of disease rather than as an effect or symptom. If you observe that children with poor reading skills watch a lot of television, you might easily assume that television interferes with their reading. In fact, excessive viewing could be a symptom. Because those children have trouble reading, they watch television instead.

STRATEGIES FOR ENHANCING CRITICAL THINKING

There is no quick method of enhancing critical thinking, but you can challenge yourself to move beyond first impressions and hasty generalizations by considering these questions:

1. **How much do you really know about this subject?** Do you fully understand the history, depth, and character of the topic? Should you learn more by conducting some research or interviewing people before making judgments?

Continued

2. **Have you looked at your topic closely?** First impressions can be striking but misleading. Examine your subject closely, asking questions, probing beneath the surface. Look for patterns; measure similarities and differences.

3. **Have you rushed to judgment?** Collect evidence but avoid drawing conclusions until you have analyzed your findings and observations.

4. **Do you separate facts from opinions?** Don't confuse facts, evidence, and data with opinions, claims, and assertions. Opinions are judgments or inferences, not facts. Facts are reliable pieces of information that can be verified by studying other sources:

   FACT: This semester a laptop, petty cash, and a VCR were taken from the tutoring lab while Sue Harper was on duty.
   OPINION: Sue Harper is a thief.

   The factual statement can be proven. Missing items can be documented. The assumption that Sue Harper is responsible remains to be proven.

5. **Are you aware of your assumptions?** Assumptions are ideas we accept or believe to be true. It is nearly impossible to divorce ourselves from what we have been taught, but you can sharpen your critical thinking skills if you acknowledge your assumptions. Avoid relying too heavily on a single assumption—IQ tests measure intelligence, poverty causes crime, television is a bad influence on children.

6. **Have you collected enough evidence?** A few statistics and quotations taken out of context may seem convincing, but they cannot be viewed as adequate proof. Make sure you collect enough evidence from a variety of sources before making judgments.

7. **Do you evaluate evidence carefully?** Do you apply common standards to evaluate the data you collect? Do you question the source of statistics or the validity of an eyewitness? The fact that you can find dozens of books written about alien abductions does not prove they occur.

CRITICAL THINKING EXERCISE

1. Review the list of topics and select one that you have strong opinions and feelings about.

the President	the war on	gun control	reality TV shows
underage	terrorism	high school	your boss
drinking	an NFL coach or	blind dates	daycare
worst teacher	player	sexual	raves
health insurance	gay rights	harassment	global warming
smokers	affirmative action	legalizing	the environment
SUVs	lotteries	marijuana	religion
your last job	cable news	cloning	rap music
suicide bombers	networks	proms	
	student loans	AIDS	
	welfare		

2. After selecting a topic write a statement summarizing your attitudes about it. Write a full paragraph or list ideas, or even words, you associate with this subject:
3. Examine your comments carefully and consider these questions:

- *What do I really know about this topic?*
- *Why do I feel this way?*
- *Would other people call my views unfairly biased?*
- *Are my views based on facts or assumptions?*
- *Can I provide sufficient evidence to support my opinion?*
- *Do I detect any logical fallacies in my response—hasty generalizations, red herrings, or mistaking a time relationship for a cause?*
- *Do I need to conduct research before I can honestly make a judgment?*
- *Are there alternative opinions? Do they have any merit?*
- *Could I organize a logical and convincing argument to persuade others to accept my point of view?*

Examining and challenging your values, ideas, and opinions improves your ability to express yourself to others and anticipate their questions and objections.

PREWRITING: PUTTING CRITICAL THINKING INTO ACTION

Writing is not only used to create a document, it also can be used to think on paper, to explore ideas, discover topics, develop details, and identify significant facts. Instead of trying to start a draft of an assignment, use writing as a way of recording and prompting critical thinking.

Writers use a number of prewriting techniques. Depending on the assignment, you may find one method more helpful than others. Although usually taught as separate methods, these prewriting strategies should not be viewed as a set of rigid procedures. Writers often blend several methods when thinking about a topic.

Prewriting Strategies

Brainstorming

Brainstorming takes many forms. Often writers start with an idea and begin making lists. The goal is to let one idea trigger another, as in a psychologist's free association exercise:

```
cars
new cars/SUVs
gas mileage
Middle East politics/oil/need for big cars?
traffic jams
commute to work
potholes
freeway
original freeway plan of 1960s/current traffic
traffic delays/stress/trapped in crowded system
freeways designed to make life easier 40 years ago have trapped people
in an obsolete system with no alternatives
```

Starting with "cars," the writer has moved through a series of ideas until she hit on a topic for a short essay, the crowded freeway system.

- Brainstorming can help you get started when you feel lost for a topic because you can easily jump from one idea to another. Even the most general or abstract starting point can identify a topic appropriate for an upcoming assignment.

Brainstorming is not limited to finding topics for academic assignments. When you know what you want to say, you can use targeted brainstorming to identify details needed to create an effective document. If you are writing an e-mail to apply for a job you saw posted on the Internet, you can use brainstorming to generate a list of details you might want to include in a cover letter and resume:

Assistant Manager – Coffee Nation

Two years' experience at Pablo's Café
Supervised four employees in manager's absence
Accounting and business courses related to retail
Completed restaurant management course UW-Whitewater
Fully familiar with Coffee Nation's products & services
Effective at motivating and training staff
Good at customer relations—helped Pablo's build repeat business
Get references from Pablo, Lucy Perez, Ted Weinstein

- Targeted brainstorming triggers ideas you might overlook if you simply start writing.

Asking Questions

Another method that sparks critical thinking is to ask questions. Write as many questions about your subject as possible. Don't pause to answer them, just list as many questions as you can:

Why do I hate commuting?
How long does it take me get home on a good day?
A bad day?
Why does it take so long?
When were the freeways designed?
Why are they so congested?
Why are there no other fast routes?
Why don't we have bus or rail service to suburbs?
How much will fixing the freeway cost?
Can new lanes be added?
Will the congestion make people lose desire to live in
suburbs and want to move back downtown?

- Asking questions forces you to think rather than simply observe. It is a useful method to test assumptions because questions ask for proof. If you list an idea such as "high school math was a waste" you simply record an opinion. Forcing yourself to ask questions like "Was high school math a waste?" or "Why do I feel high school math was a waste?" prompts a more thoughtful response.

- Posing questions can quickly identify topics requiring further research.

Freewriting

In freewriting you record your thoughts, ideas, impressions, and feelings without stopping or pausing to edit for spelling, grammar, punctuation, or even logic. Don't confuse freewriting with writing a rough draft of an essay—it is a method of discovering ideas. Freewriting is not unlike talking to yourself. It has no direction; it can skip from one topic to another without rational transitions; it may contain contradictory statements. Freewriting produces "running prose," like the tape recording of a rambling telephone conversation. The goal is to sketch out ideas as fast as you can.

Sit down with a piece of paper or at a computer and start writing. Some experts suggest writing nonstop for at least five minutes. If you can't think of anything to write, draw O's and X's or type gibberish. The main thing is to keep the process going until you can think of something to say. Let one idea remind you of another. Remember, there are no bad ideas.

Having spent a frustrating afternoon locked in bumper-to-bumper traffic on the expressway, a student came home and rapidly recorded her thoughts for an upcoming comparison essay:

The expressways built in the 1960s were supposed to liberate us from traffic jams. An early brochure my dad has shows the neat ribbons of conrete stretching in a planned set of spokes from the center city to the suburbs. "From Center City to Centerville in 15 minutes" (mayor's quote). And so the inter-urban trolleys were scrapped and their rails torn out. Bus routes were dropped and the freeways were built. And maybe for a few years people cokuld actually comute from Brookfield to downtown in fifteen minutes. x x x x x x x x x x x x x x x

But no one could forsee the endless suburban sprawl of malls, subdidivisons, industrials parks not to mention the new airport. By the 1980s the expressways were busy, bythe 90s clogged, and now there hopless. Downtown housing is eiter undesirable or unaffordable. Middleclass people have to live in the suburbs. But the jobs remain downtown. So with two parents working and kids attending separate schools families have two, three, even four cars, all clogging the espressays.

In 1940 it probably took a guy forty-five minutes to get from rural Centerville to City Hall on a bumpy two lane county road. Now on the expressway it takes just as long on a six lane potholed freeway system nearly the end of its fifty year lifespan.

They say it will cost almost a billion dollars and three years to fix the potholes, upgrade the bridges, and redo the crumbling ramps. When it is all done it will take an hour to get form Centerville to City Hall, except maybe the ride will be smoother. Like a lot of people who live in the suburbs and work downtown I feel condemned. I wish there was another option. At least on a train I could read or take a nap instead of wasting my time crawling at 10mph past signs warning me the speed limit is 70.

- Freewriting allows one idea to trigger another without your worrying about making logical connections.
- Freewriting can help you overcome writer's block. Having the freedom to write anything, even meaningless symbols, can help you avoid feeling that you have to produce flawless prose whenever you write.
- If writing complete sentences becomes time-consuming, just list key words or make notes. List or cluster ideas to save time. Don't feel obligated to write in complete sentences.

Clustering

Clustering is a visual method of prewriting. Instead of writing down ideas in whole sentences or generating lists, you map or sketch out ideas to establish patterns and relationships:

Freeways

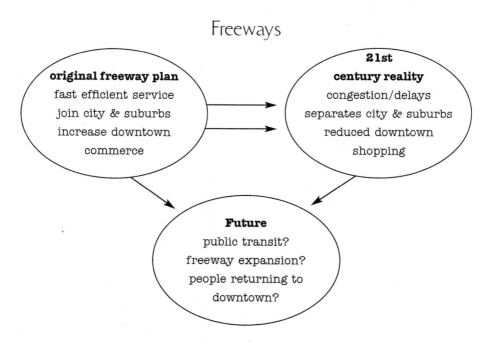

- Clustering assists writers who are visually oriented. Some people find it easier to think critically by placing ideas in columns or charts to show relationships, dramatize advantages and disadvantages, or explore causes and effects.

Remember, you can easily blend different techniques. You might begin by brainstorming, then freewrite to explore a certain idea, next pose some questions to identify areas that need research, and then use clustering to contrast opposing ideas.

Writing Exercise

Select one of the topics below and explore it using one or more methods of prewriting.

cell phones	drunk driving laws	talk shows	online dating
worst job	Iraq	high school bullies	video games
teen fashions	athletes as role models	euthanasia	racial profiling
singles bars	diets	airport security	Internet stalking
credit cards	car insurance	death penalty	child support

Critical Reading

*If reading is to accomplish anything more
than passing time, it must be active.*
Mortimer Adler

In most college courses you read for knowledge, highlighting key terms, dates, facts, and theories that may appear on upcoming tests. When you read for pleasure, you probably don't take notes at all. You allow yourself to be taken into the writer's world, focusing on a story's characters and plot. Reading a magazine or newspaper article to learn about stocks or a new diet, you skim through familiar material to concentrate on new information.

Reading in a writing class is different. Few instructors are likely to "test" you on the content of the articles they assign. Rather, they expect you to examine an article to appreciate *how* it is written—how the writer presents and supports a thesis, organizes details, uses logic, selects words, and addresses the needs and concerns of readers.

READING WITH A WRITER'S EYE

When most people see a movie they allow themselves to be drawn into the story, to enjoy the action, laugh at jokes, or feel compassion for a character in crisis. But a film student watching the same movie studies how the director uses lighting, editing, and camera angles to create a scene. A drama student observes how an actor delivers a line or uses a gesture to establish a character.

As a composition student you need to read with a "writer's eye." Reading gives you the opportunity to watch other writers at work. When you read, note the way writers use words, form sentences, and develop paragraphs. Study how they limit topics, present ideas, address controversial issues, and indicate transitions. Read to discover techniques you can use in your own assignments:

- How did the author limit the subject?
- How did the writer arouse interest in the topic?

- What sentence opens the essay?
- What details did the writer include, and what details did he or she omit?
- How did the author present background information?
- What audience is the writer addressing?
- Where did the writer place the thesis statement?
- What kind of support is used?
- How did the writer organize ideas?
- How does word choice affect the tone and style?
- What thought, image, question, or fact did the author choose for the conclusion?

READING CRITICALLY

Critical reading takes place in stages. At first glance, it might seem to be a long process, but in fact, following these steps can maximize your time and help you focus on the most important elements of anything you read, including the essays in this text.

First Reading

1. **Look ahead and skim selections.** Do not wait until the night before a class discussion to read assignments. Check your syllabus and skim through upcoming readings to get a general impression. Often, if you think about the authors and their topics, you can approach the essay more critically.
2. **Study the head note and introduction.** Consider the author, the issue, and what you already know about the subject. Note the original source of the essay. What type of readers does the writer seem to be addressing?
3. **Suspend judgment.** Try to put your personal views aside as you read. Even if you disagree with the author's choice of topic, tone, or opinion, read the essay objectively. Remember, your goal is to understand *how* the writer states his or her point. Even if you reject an author's thesis, you can still learn useful techniques.
4. **Consider the title.** Titles often provide clues about the author's attitude toward his or her subject. Does the title label the essay, state a thesis, pose a question, or use a creative phrase to attract attention?
5. **Read the entire work.** Complete the entire essay in one sitting if you can. Do not pause to look up an unfamiliar word at this stage. Instead, try to get the "big picture."
6. **Focus on understanding the writer's main point.** If possible, summarize the writer's thesis in your own words.

7. **Jot down your first impressions.** What do you think of this work? Do you like it? If so, why? If you find it dull, disturbing, or silly, ask yourself why. What is lacking? How did the author fail in your eyes?

Put the essay aside, allowing it to cool. If possible, let two or three days pass before returning to the assignment. If the assignment is due the next day, read the selection early in the day and then turn to other work or run an errand, so you can come back to it with a fresh outlook.

Second Reading

1. **Review your first impressions.** Determine if your attitudes are based on biases or personal preferences rather than the writer's ability. Realize that an essay that supports your views is not necessarily well written. If you disagree with the author's thesis, try to put your opinions aside to objectively evaluate how well the writer presented his or her point of view. Don't allow your personal views to cloud your critical thinking. Appreciating an author's writing ability does not require you to accept his or her opinions or values.

2. **Read with a pen in your hand.** Make notes and underline passages that strike you as important, memorable, interesting, funny, odd, or disturbing. Reading with a pen will prompt you to write, to be an active reader rather than a passive consumer of words.

3. **Look up unfamiliar words.** Paying attention to words can increase your vocabulary and enhance your appreciation of connotations.

4. **Analyze passages you found difficult or confusing during the first reading.** In many instances a second reading can help you understand complex passages. If you still have difficulty understanding the writer's point, ask why. Would other readers also have problems comprehending the meaning? Could ideas be stated more directly?

5. **Review any questions at the end of the selection.** Considering the following questions can help you focus on a closer, more analytical reading of the work. The questions are arranged in three groups:

Understanding Meaning:
   What is the writer's goal?
   What is the thesis?
   What audience is the writer addressing?
   What is the author trying to share with his or her readers?

Analyzing Strategy:
   How effective is the title?
   How does the writer introduce the essay?

What evidence supports the thesis?
How does the writer organize ideas?
Where does the author use paragraph breaks?
What role does the writer play? Is the writer's approach subjective or objective?
How does the writer address possible objections or differing opinions?
How does the writer conclude the essay?
Does the author use any special techniques?

Evaluating Language:

How does the writer use words?
What does the language reveal about the intended readers?
What connotations do the words have?
How do the words establish the writer's tone?

6. **Summarize your responses in a point or two for class discussion.** Consider how you will express your opinions of the essay to fellow students. Be prepared to back up your remarks by citing passages in the text.

7. **Most importantly, focus on what this essay can teach you about writing.** How can this writer's style, way of organizing ideas, or word choice enrich your own writing? Though you may not wish to imitate everything you see, you can learn techniques to broaden your personal composing style.

8. **Think of how writers resolve problems you have encountered.** If you have trouble making an outline and organizing ideas, study how the essays in this book are arranged. If your instructor returns papers with comments about vague thesis statements and lack of focus, examine how the writers in this book generate controlling ideas.

Before Class Discussion

1. **Before class discussion of an assigned essay, review the reading and your notes.** Identify your main reactions to the piece. What do you consider the essay's strongest or weakest points?

2. **Ask fellow students about their reactions to the writing.** Determine if their responses to the writer's thesis, tone, approach, and technique match yours. If their reactions differ from yours, review your notes to get a fresh perspective.

3. **Be prepared to ask questions.** Ask your instructor about unfamiliar techniques or passages you find confusing.

Read the following essay by Scott Simon and note how he presents and supports his point of view:

SCOTT SIMON

Scott Simon is a war correspondent and reporter, but he is best known to listeners of National Public Radio as the host of "Weekend Edition with Scott Simon."

Why Even Pacifists Support This War

OVERVIEW: *This essay appeared shortly after the September 11, 2001, terrorist attacks against the World Trade Center and the Pentagon. As you read Simon's argument, consider if subsequent events have altered the thoughts and emotions the attacks produced. Is the idea of a war against terrorism as popular now as it was in late 2001? Why or why not?*

1 Introduction Pacifists often commit the same mistake as generals: They prepare for the last war, not the next one.

2 Many of the peace activists I have seen trying to rouse opposition to today's war against terrorism remind me of a Halloween parade. They put on old, familiar-looking protest masks—against American imperialism, oppression and violence—that bear no resemblance to the real demons haunting us now.

3 appeal of pacifism Pacifism has never been exactly popular. But when I became a Quaker as an adolescent in the late 1960s, pacifism seemed to offer a compelling alternative to the perpetuity of brute force. Mahatma Gandhi had overthrown an empire, and Martin Luther King had overturned a racial tyranny with nonviolent marches, fasts and boycotts that were nervy, ennobling and effective.

4 Pacifism seemed to offer a chance for survival to a generation that had been stunted by the fear of nuclear extinction.

5 Simon's roles as Quaker and war reporter I worked as a war reporter, but I never saw a conflict between this and being a Quaker. If my reporting was sometimes drawn more to human details than to the box-score kind of war coverage, those details struck me as critical to explaining war. I never covered a conflict—whether in Central America, the Caribbean, Africa or the Middle East—that seriously shook my religious convictions.

6 In fact, most conflicts seemed to prove how war was rotten, wasteful and useless. El Salvador's civil war killed 70,000 people over nine years. It

was hard to see how the political compromise that ended the conflict could not have been reached after just six months.

But in the 1990s, I covered the Balkans. In Sarajevo, Srebrenica and Kosovo, I confronted the logical flaw (or perhaps I should say the fatal flaw) of non-violent resistance: All the best people can be killed by all the worst ones.

I had never believed that pacifism had all the answers; neither does militarism. About half of all draft age Quakers enlisted in World War II, believing that whatever wisdom pacifism had to give the world, it could not defeat the murderous schemes of Adolf Hitler and his cohorts.

It seems to me that in confronting the forces that attacked the World Trade Center and the Pentagon, American pacifists have no sane alternative now but to support war. I don't consider this reprisal or revenge, but self-defense: protecting the world from further attacks by destroying those who would launch them.

Some peace activists, their judgment still hobbled by shock, seem to believe that the attacks against New York and Washington were natural disasters: terrible, unpredictable whirlwinds that struck once and will not re-occur.

This is wrong. We know now that there has been an ongoing violent campaign aimed at bringing down diverse nations, with none being more gloriously speckled than the United States. People who try to hold certain American policies or culture responsible are trying to decorate the crimes of psychotics with synthetic political significance.

In 1933, the Oxford Student Union conducted a famous debate over whether it was moral for Britons to fight for king and country. The exquisite intellects of that leading university reviewed the many ways in which British colonialism exploited and oppressed the world. They cited the ways in which vengeful demands made of Germany in the wake of World War I had helped to kindle nationalism and fascism. They saw no moral difference between Western colonialism and world fascism.

The Oxford Union ended that debate with this famous proclamation: "Resolved, that we will in no circumstances fight for king and country."

Von Ribbentrop sent back the good news to Germany's new chancellor, Hitler: The West will not fight for its own survival. Its finest minds will justify a silent surrender.

In short, the best-educated young people of their time could not tell the difference between the deficiencies of their own nation, in which liberty and democracy were cornerstones, and a dictatorship founded on racism, tyranny and fear.

And what price would those who urge reconciliation today pay for peace?

17   Should Americans impose a unitary religious state, throw women out of school and work and rob other religious groups of their rights so that we have the kind of society the attackers accept? Do pacifists really want to live in the kind of world that the terrorists who hit the World Trade Center and Pentagon would make?

18   Pacifists do not need any lectures about risking their lives to stop wickedness. Quakers resisted slavery by smuggling out slaves when even Abraham Lincoln tried to appease the Confederacy. Pacifists sneaked refugee Jews out of Germany when England and the U.S. were still trying to placate Hitler. Many conscientious objectors have served bravely in gritty and unglamorous tasks that aided the U.S. in time of war.

19   But those of us who have been pacifists must admit that it has been our blessing to live in a nation in which other citizens have been willing to risk their lives to defend our dissent.

20   The war against terrorism does not shove American power into calls on America's military strength in a global crisis in which peaceful solutions are not apparent.

21   Only American (and British) power can stop more killing in the world's skyscrapers, pizza parlors, embassies, bus stations, ships and airplanes. Pacifists, like most Americans, would like to change their country in a thousand ways. And the blasts of Sept. 11 should remind American pacifists that they live in that one place on the planet where change—in fact, peaceful conclusion change—seems most possible.

22   <u>It is better to sacrifice our ideals than to expect others to die for them.</u>

 E-WRITING: Exploring Writing Resources Online

The Internet provides an ever-growing range of information about reading. Using a search engine like Google or Alta Vista, enter the terms "reading strategies," "critical reading," and "reading techniques" to locate useful information.

InfoTrac® College Edition

For additional resources go to InfoTrac College Edition, your online research library, at http://infotrac.thomsonlearning.com.

1. Enter the terms "reading strategies" and "critical reading" in the Subject Guide.
2. Enter the terms "reading skills," "improving reading comprehension," and "reading techniques" using Keywords.
3. Review online articles from current issues of major magazines and newspapers to practice reading skills.
4. Print copies of selected articles for future rereading and review.

STRATEGIES FOR CRITICAL READING

As you read selections in the text, consider these questions:

1. **What is the writer's goal?** Even writers exploring the same topic, such as describing an event or comparing two people, have different intentions. What is the purpose of the essay—to raise questions, motivate people to take action, change readers' perceptions?

2. **What is the thesis?** What is the writer's main idea? Is the thesis explicitly stated, developed throughout the essay, or only implied? Can you state the thesis in your own words?

3. **What evidence does the writer provide to support the thesis?** Does the writer use personal observations, narratives, facts, statistics, or examples to support his or her conclusions?

4. **How does the writer organize the essay?** How does he or she introduce readers to the topic, develop ideas, arrange information, conclude the essay? How does the writer use modes, such as comparison, process, and definition?

5. **Who are the intended readers?** What does the original source of the document tell you about its intended audience? Does the writer direct the essay to a particular group or a general readership? What terms or references are used? Are technical or uncommon terms defined? What knowledge does the writer seem to assume readers already possess?

6. **How successful is the writing in context?** Does the writer achieve his or her goals while respecting the needs of the reader and the conventions of the discipline or situation? Are there particular considerations that cause the writer to "break" the rules of "good writing"? Why?

7. **What can you learn about writing?** What does this writer teach you about using words, writing sentences, developing paragraphs? Are there any techniques you can use in future assignments?

STRATEGIES FOR USING PREWRITING

1. After completing prewriting, set your notes aside and let them cool. Work on other assignments, read, work out, or run an errand so that later you can return to your work with greater objectivity.

2. If you are responding to an assignment, review your instructor's directions carefully.

3. Review your prewriting notes, keeping the requirements of the assignment in mind.

4. Highlight significant ideas. Cross off repeated or irrelevant details.

5. Try to develop a topic or a list of topics suited to your assignment.

6. Narrow the topic to something suited to the paper.

7. Develop a thesis statement—your main idea. Remember a thesis is not simply a narrowed topic but a point of view, an assertion, an opinion.

8. List evidence to support the thesis.

9. Continue prewriting if needed to refine your thesis or identify additional evidence.

10. Create an outline to guide the writing of your first draft.

 E-WRITING: Exploring Critical Thinking Online

The Internet presents a range of sources dedicated to critical thinking, ranging from sites maintained by academic organizations to those created by individual teachers posting information for their students.

1. Enter *"critical thinking"* as a search term in a general search engine such as Yahoo, Alta Vista, or Google to locate current websites dedicated to critical thinking.

2. Locate the online version of a national or local newspaper and review recent editorials. Can you detect any lapses in critical thinking? Do any editorials rely on hasty generalizations, anecdotal evidence, faulty comparisons, circular reasoning, or borrowed authorities?

3. For more dramatic examples of discovery errors in critical thinking, use search terms to locate sites about controversial topics. Review their arguments for lapses in critical thinking. Do you think these errors are accidental or deliberate?

4. To learn more about a specific problem in critical thinking, use one or more of the
   following as search terms:

coincidence	anecdotal evidence	post hoc	circular reasoning
red herrings	guilt by association	hasty generalizations	fact and opinion

InfoTrac® College Edition

For additional resources go to InfoTrac College Edition, your online research
library, at http://infotrac.thomsonlearning.com.

1. Enter "critical thinking," "logical fallacies," "hasty generalizations," "guilt by
   association," and "fact and opinion" as search terms.

2. Review several online articles on controversial topics for errors in critical thinking.

Conducting Research

The research paper is, in the fullest sense, a discovery and an education that leads you beyond texts, beyond a library, and encourages you to investigate on your own.

Audrey J. Roth

WHAT IS RESEARCH?

The words *research paper* on a syllabus can instill anxiety and dread. Perhaps you found writing term papers in high school a frustrating and time-consuming chore. Even if you received good grades in the past, you may feel wholly unprepared for the level of work expected in college. For most students research papers imply endless hours spent locating sources, photocopying articles, downloading databases, taking notes, selecting facts, organizing quotations, writing, and rewriting—all while trying to remember when to use endnotes.

Your ability to write effective research papers will greatly determine your success in college. In some courses the research project accounts for more than half the final grade. Instructors assign research papers because, unlike objective tests, they measure your ability to solve problems, apply knowledge, gather evidence, and interpret data.

Learning how to write a good research paper will not only improve your academic performance but also sharpen the critical thinking skills needed in most careers. Although few people write traditional research papers once they leave college, almost every professional uses the same methods to produce annual reports, market studies, product evaluations, proposals, and letters. Executives, administrators, attorneys, entrepreneurs, and scientists must base their decisions and recommendations on information. The ability to locate accurate sources, evaluate evidence, and interpret findings is essential for success in any field.

Common Misconceptions

Before undertaking a research paper, it is important to understand what a research paper is *not*. Many students work very hard collecting material and writing pages of text only to receive low grades because the paper they produce fails to meet the instructor's requirements. Even students who do well on research papers often make the project more burdensome and time-consuming than needed.

A research paper is not a summary of everything you can find about your topic.   The goal in writing a research paper is not to present a collection of facts and quotations "about" a topic but to state a clear thesis supported by evidence. Although it is important to survey information, using twenty sources instead of ten will not necessarily improve the quality of your paper. The goal of a research paper is to present carefully selected evidence that supports your thesis.

A research paper does not simply repeat what others have written. A research paper is more than a string of related quotations and summaries. It is important to qualify evidence, to critique the quality and quantity of the sources you select. Research writers not only collect evidence but also evaluate and interpret it. The focus of a research paper is your thesis and commentary—not pages of text you have cut and pasted from the Internet.

A research paper does not merely support a preconceived point of view.   Honest research begins with a topic or question. You should only reach a conclusion and develop a thesis after carefully examining the evidence. Taking the ideas of others out of context to support your position on abortion or the death penalty is not research.

A research paper does not include the ideas of others without documentation.   Including the ideas and words of others in your text without attribution is plagiarism. Whenever you add facts, quotations, and summaries of outside sources, you must identify them.

CONDUCTING RESEARCH: AN OVERVIEW

Writing a research paper can be made less intimidating and less arduous if you break the process into key steps:

- Understand the scope of the assignment.
- Select an appropriate topic.
- Conduct preliminary research.
- Limit the topic and develop a working thesis.
- Create a timeline.
- Collect and evaluate relevant evidence.

Understand the Scope of the Assignment

Some instructors assign topics for research papers, but most professors provide students with directions or guidelines, allowing them to select topics. Students may be required to use a certain number of sources, present evidence in a specific manner, or address a particular issue:

Write an eight- to ten-page research paper using APA documentation that compares past and present treatments of a common psychological disorder. Your sources must include at least two professional interviews.

Analyze a critical theme, character, or technique used by the author of one of the works we have studied in this class. Do not summarize the work or repeat what you may have presented in your oral report. Your paper should be six to eight pages long, include a minimum of three electronic sources, and documented in MLA style.

Select a noted trial, Supreme Court decision, or scandal and examine its lasting impact on the law, American institutions, or perceptions of justice. Your paper should be ten pages long and documented in APA style.

- **It is important to fully understand all the requirements of an assignment and refer to them throughout the process.** Perhaps the most common mistake students make is failing to address the needs of the assignment. Once you begin looking up sources and examining data, you can be easily led astray and write an interesting paper that fails to meet the instructor's requirements. The psychology student writing about schizophrenia may be impressed by some recent medical articles and write a thorough research paper outlining genetic factors. Though well written and properly documented, if it fails to draw a comparison between past and present treatments and does not include interviews, the paper may be wholly unacceptable.
- **Ask your instructor for clarification of any points you find confusing.** If your instructor does not supply handouts, take careful notes to record specific requirements and directions. If your instructor does not assign topics, you may wish to ask for suggestions. Ask your instructor which topics to avoid.
- **Make copies of any instructor handouts or notes and keep them next to your computer or in your purse or briefcase for quick reference.** Refer to these guidelines when visiting the library or searching the Internet. Make sure your research remains focused on sources that address the needs of the assignment.

Select an Appropriate Topic

The first step in writing a research paper is selecting a topic or topics. Until you begin collecting evidence, you may not be sure if the subjects you start with are workable. Often, subjects that you might find interesting at first become unmanageable because sources are lacking or too numerous to handle.

STRATEGIES FOR SELECTING A TOPIC

1. **Select a topic that matches the assignment.** If your instructor requires you to include personal interviews, you may find it difficult to locate people who can provide insights on highly specialized issues. You may find local mental health professionals or volunteers who can tell you about depression, addiction, or common mental illnesses. But it may be difficult to locate anyone with knowledge of bimodal processing.

2. **Select a topic that interests you.** If you don't really care about your subject, you may find it difficult to sustain a long research effort. If you choose a topic that you have little knowledge about, you will have to conduct extensive background research. Brainstorm to discover if your existing knowledge and experiences apply to the assignment. Discuss possible topics with your instructor or friends and ask for suggestions.

3. **Consider your long-term goals.** Writing a research paper offers an opportunity to explore issues and subjects related to personal and career goals. Many doctoral dissertations and business proposals began as research projects. In addition to fulfilling a course requirement, your research may help shape your career goals or locate information you can use in your job or business. Make sure that your personal interests do not conflict with the goals of the assignment—refer to the instructor's guidelines to keep your project on track.

4. **Select a topic that is flexible.** Until you begin researching, you cannot tell how much information is readily available. Think of your topic as an accordion, something that may have to be compressed or expanded.

Continued

5. **Be willing to alter or reject topics.** Your first topic is only a starting point. If you find it difficult to work with, drop it and select another. Do not feel obligated to stick with something unless required by your instructor. Use prewriting techniques like clustering, brainstorming, and asking questions to develop new approaches to your topic.

6. **Select more than one topic to start.** At this point no decision is final. Until you begin investigating ideas, you may not know if a topic will be suitable. If you are unsure which topic to pursue, sketch out two or three for preliminary research.

Topics to Avoid

- **Topics that rely on a single source.** Research papers coordinate information from several sources. If you select an event covered in one news story or a process explained by a single set of instructions, you will not be able to achieve a major goal of a research paper. Check with your instructor if you are interested in a topic with only a single source.

- **Highly controversial topics—unless you can develop a new approach.** It is unlikely you can write anything about capital punishment or abortion that has not already been stated—unless you look at the issue from a unique perspective. You might research murder rates, comparing states with or without the death penalty, or examine Buddhist views of abortion. Controversial subjects may be difficult to research because many sources can be biased. Discuss your topic with your instructor and ask for recommended approaches or alternative subjects.

- **New topics.** Events or issues that have just happened may be difficult to research because little has been published except news reports and fragmentary comments. A quick Internet search might locate the amount of reliable material currently available.

- **Topics lacking credible sources.** Conducting research about UFOs, psychic phenomena, and alternative medicine can be difficult because sources may be anecdotal and unscientific. Avoid "conspiracy"-related issues. By their nature, these topics resist objective investigation. A reference librarian can suggest sources or a new topic.

- **Popular topics.** As when writing about a controversial topic, it may be difficult to find something new to say about an issue many students have written about. Popular issues may be hard to research because many of the books may already be checked out of the library.

- **Topics difficult to narrow or expand.** Until you begin discovering sources, you will not know how complex your task will be. If you select a topic that resists alterations, you may be forced to reject it in favor of a more manageable subject.

Conduct Preliminary Research

Once you have selected a topic or topics, you are ready to explore your subject. Your goal at this point is not to locate specific sources for your research paper but to survey the field of knowledge, get a sense of the discipline, identify schools of thought, and research trends, areas of conflict, and new discoveries.

STRATEGIES FOR CONDUCTING PRELIMINARY RESEARCH

1. **Review textbooks.** Textbooks generally offer brief overviews of subjects, but they also often include endnotes, bibliographies, and footnotes that can direct you to books and articles about specific issues.

2. **Survey encyclopedia articles.** A good encyclopedia will present background information that may help you get a fuller view of your subject. Online and CD versions have a search feature that allows you to type in keywords to generate a list of related articles.

3. **Review specialized encyclopedias, dictionaries, and directories.** A general encyclopedia such as *The Encyclopedia Britannica* can offer only brief commentaries on subjects and will not include minor people, events, or subjects. The reference room of your library will likely have specialized encyclopedias. The *Britannica Encyclopedia of American Art*, for example, might offer a multipage article about an artist not even mentioned in general encyclopedias.

4. **Review indexes, databases, and abstracts.** Available in print, online, or on CD-ROM, these are valuable tools in conducting research. Databases list articles. Many provide abstracts that briefly summarize articles, usually in a single paragraph. Still other databases are especially useful because they include the entire article in addition to abstracts. If the complete text is available, you may download and save it to a disk for later reading and note taking. Skimming abstracts allows you to quickly review a dozen articles in the time it would take to locate a journal and find a single article. Abstracts not only list the source of the full article but also indicate its length and special features such as photographs or tables. Sources like *Chemical Abstracts*, *Psychological Abstracts*, and *Criminal Justice Abstracts* provide summaries in specific disciplines. Many libraries

Continued

---

subscribe to online services, such as InfoTrac College Edition, that list articles from thousands of general, business, and scholarly newspapers, journals, and magazines.

Consult a librarian for assistance in identifying those articles for which the database includes the complete text. By their nature, abstracts of articles have limited usefulness. Full-text articles, on the other hand, will be invaluable after you've left the library.

Also, ask a librarian if you can access the library's databases from a remote site (for example, at home, in your dorm room, or from a laptop with Internet connection). This convenience provides countless advantages. Note: If this option is available, you'll likely need a current user name and password to gain access.

5. **Conduct an Internet search.** In addition to specific databases such as InfoTrac College Edition, you can use a number of popular search engines such as Alta Vista, Yahoo!, or Google to search for sources on the Internet. Each of these engines or search tools can access millions of sites. These tools offer Web guides that organize sites by categories such as "arts and humanities," "education," or "news and media." You can also enter key words to generate specific lists.

Students unfamiliar with conducting Internet searches are often frustrated by the overwhelming list of unrelated "hits" they receive. Entering Martin Luther King, Jr. may generate thousands of sites about Billy *Martin, Martin Luther,* and *King* George III.

Search engines usually provide tools to refine your search.

- Check the spelling of your search terms, especially names.
- Make the search words as specific as possible.
- Follow the search engine's directions to narrow your search. It will give you specific ways to include or exclude terms in your search.
- Internet searches may locate home pages of sites with numerous sources and direct links to related sites.
- You can find the latest update for a Web page by entering **javascript:alert(document.lastModified)** in the Internet Explorer address box.
- If you find it difficult to locate useful sources, ask a reference librarian for assistance.

E-RESEARCH ACTIVITY: Exploring Preliminary
Research Online

Explore the research sources available at your library or through online databases.

1. Determine which catalog system your library uses. Use the card catalog or computer catalog to look up *Lord of the Rings*. What is the novel's call number? Where is it located in the library?

2. Examine the list of online databases available in your library.

3. Search a business database for a company you have worked for or done business with (such as Taco Bell, Coca-Cola, Home Depot, Bath and Body, or Proctor and Gamble).

4. Use the Medline database to generate a list of articles about a medical problem you or a family member have experienced (for example, carpal tunnel syndrome, diabetes, or arthritis).

5. Use a general database like Reader's Guide, InfoTrac, or Infoseek to obtain a list of recent articles on one or more of the following topics:

   caffeine   federal witness protection program
   Alzheimer's disease   high-definition television
   the Patriot Act   Hubble Space Telescope

6. Using one of the articles you identified in Research Activity 5, save the file to a disk and then print a hard copy of the first page of the text.

7. Send the file you created in Research Activity 6 as an e-mail attachment to your own e-mail address for later retrieval. This method might be necessary if you locate an article on a database but have no way to save it to your disk (perhaps you've forgotten it or it has become corrupted).

8. Use a search engine like Lycos, Yahoo!, Google, or Alta Vista to search for websites about one or more of the following topics:

   Parkinson's disease   scuba diving
   Sandra Day O'Connor   Yellowstone National Park
   dive sites in the Florida Keys   automobile child restraint seats

   Follow the search engine directions to limit your search and reduce the number of irrelevant sites.

A Note on Conducting Preliminary Research

Remember, your goal at this point is to simply survey the field and get an overall feel for your subject. Don't get bogged down with details or allow yourself to become overwhelmed by the complexity or number of sources.

- Determine if there is sufficient material on your subject to work with.
- Look for ways of limiting your topic.

- Identify patterns in the data—conflicting points of view, clusters of related articles, key figures or authors, current theories, or research trends.
- Allow sources to direct you to new topics or new approaches to your subject.

Continually refer to your instructor's guidelines to keep your search on track.

Limit the Topic and Develop a Working Thesis

After surveying the field of knowledge, you can consider whether your topic is worth pursuing. If you cannot find enough material or if the sources are too diverse or scattered, you may wish to consider a new subject. In most instances, the preliminary material you have located may help you further limit your topic:

Orwell's *1984*

Loss of Freedom Predicted by Orwell in *1984*

Role of Technology in Orwell's *1984*

Orwell and the Loss of Nature in *1984*

Famous Trials

Role of Media in High Profile Trials

Leopold and Loeb Case

Role of the Press in the Leopold and Loeb Case

Asking questions can help target your paper and prevent you from simply summarizing the work or the ideas of others:

What effect does the loss of nature have on humanity in *1984?*

Did media coverage affect the outcome of the Leopold and Loeb case?

At this point you may be able to develop a working thesis, a starting point for your research paper. Although it may be general and subject to change, the working thesis moves beyond a narrowed topic or question to make a tentative statement:

Orwell considered contact with nature essential to individual liberty.

Excessive media coverage influenced the outcome of the Leopold and Loeb case.

A working thesis is a tentative statement subject to change. It is a tool to guide your research; keep an open mind and be willing to alter your opinion.

Create a Timeline

In writing an essay examination, it is important to keep your eye on the clock to prevent running out of time and leaving critical questions unanswered. Similarly, when you begin a long research project, it is important to carefully budget your time and resources. In developing a long paper, make sure you devote enough time for each stage in the writing process. Don't spend six weeks gathering materials and try to write, revise, edit, and proofread a ten-page paper over a weekend.

- **Note the due date and work backward to create a schedule allowing sufficient time for each stage in the writing process.**

May 10	Paper due
May 5	Target date for completion
May 1	Final draft prepared for final editing and proofreading
April 25	Second draft completed
April 15	First draft completed for revision and rewriting
April 10	Final outline completed, final thesis
April 5	Research completed and sources selected
March 15	Topic narrowed, working thesis, and research initiated
March 10	Topic selected and preliminary research started
March 5	Research project assigned

- **Chart your progress on a calendar to keep on track.**
- **Establish cutoff dates for major stages in the process.** If you cannot find enough material by a fixed date, talk with your instructor and consider changing topics. If you find too much material, narrow your topic.
- **Don't allow the research stage to expand past a specific date.** Keep the scope of the assignment and the length of the paper in mind to guide the quantity of material you collect. Online databases and the Internet can make research seem almost unlimited. Stay focused on your topic and the professor's instructions.

Collect and Evaluate Relevant Evidence

The type of evidence you will need to support your thesis will depend on the discipline, the topic, and the scope of the assignment. In most instances you will use *secondary sources*—expert opinions, statistics, printed interviews, historical documents, critical interpretations, and experimental results found in books, in magazines, and online. A literary paper will focus on a story or novel, biographical material about the author, and critical interpretations. An economics paper on a recent market trend may examine stock market statistics and comments by experts.

Computerized Catalogs

Most libraries use electronic catalogs that list their holdings of books, magazines, videos, and other sources. The exact instructions for using a computer will vary slightly. Most systems provide onscreen directions to locate specific works by their author or title. If you do not have a particular source in mind, you can enter a subject or topic:

Leopold and Loeb

LIST OF ITEMS   12 ITEMS MATCH YOUR SEARCH

ITEM	-AUTHOR-	TITLE	
1	Bellak, Leopold, 1916–	The schizophrenic syndrome, Leo	1967
2	Busch, Francis X	Prisoners at the bar: an accou	1952
3		Compulsion [videorecording]	1995
4	Darrow, Clarence, 1857–	Clarence Darrow pleas in defen	1926
5	Darrow, Clarence, 1857–	The plea of Clarence Darrow in	1924
6	DeFord, Miriam Allen 18	Murderers sane and mad	1965
7	Geis, Gilbert	Crimes of the century: from Leo	1998
8	Higdon, Hal	The crime of the century	1975
9	Levin, Meyer, 1905–	Compulsion—New York, Simon	1956
10	Loeb, Leo, 1869–	The venom of Heloderma	1913
11	McKernan, Maureen	The amazing crime and trial	1924
12	Vaughn, Betty Ann Erick	The forensic speaking in the	1948

By highlighting or entering the number of the source, you can access specific information about it:

AUTHOR	Higdon, Hal
TITLE	The crime of the century: the Leopold and Loeb case/ by Hal Higdon.
	—New York: Putnam, c 1975
	(AA C8080)
LOCATION	College Library Main Book Collection 3rd Floor West, Room 3191
CALL NO.	HV6245 H46

STATUS   Not checked out

FORMAT   380 p., [8] leaves of plates: ill; 24cm

NOTES   Includes index
                 Bibliography: O. 368

                 ISBN: 0399114912
                 OCLC NUMBER: 01801383

Many computerized catalogs are linked to other libraries so you can search
for sources located at other campuses or in local public libraries.

Locating Periodicals

Libraries refer to magazines and journals as *periodicals* or *serials*. You can locate a magazine or a newspaper in the catalog or *serials holding list*. But this
will simply explain where *Newsweek* or the *New York Times* is located in the
building, either in bound volumes or on microfilm. To find which articles
and issues to search for, you have to consult specific databases. Databases
list articles under key words. The *MLA Bibliography*, for instance, lists articles about literature and authors:

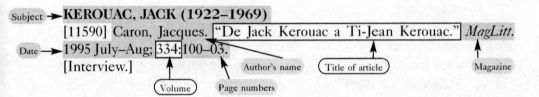

Subject → **KEROUAC, JACK (1922–1969)**
[11590] Caron, Jacques. "De Jack Kerouac a Ti-Jean Kerouac." *MagLitt.*
Date → 1995 July–Aug; 334:100–03.
[Interview.]   Author's name   Title of article   Magazine
                         Volume   Page numbers

Fiction
[11590] Oates, Joyce Carol; Dauzat, Pierre-Emmanuel, translator. "Au bout de
la route." *MagLitt.* 1995 July–Aug; 334: 96–99.

Letters
[11591] "Letters from Jack Kerouac to Ed White, 1947–68." *MissR.* 1994;
17(3): 107–60 [Includes letters (1947–1968) to White, Ed.]

Prose/Some of the Dharma
[11592] Sampas, John, foreword; Stanford, David, ed. and introd. *Some of
the Dharma.* New York, NY: Viking; 1997. 420pp. ISBN 0-670-84877-8 [And
poetry. Edition.]

SELECTING AND EVALUATING SOURCES

Database and Internet searches may provide you with hundreds, even thousands, of sources. Before you begin printing or photocopying, consider the type and number of sources needed. Without planning a list, you may waste a great deal of time collecting sources that may be interesting but unsuited to your paper.

STRATEGIES FOR SELECTING AND EVALUATING SOURCES

1. **List the types of sources needed to support your working thesis.** Review the assignment, instructor's directions, your preliminary research, and your working thesis to develop a list of needed sources:

Working Thesis:
Orwell considered contact with nature essential to individual liberty.

   Sources needed:
   Orwell's attitudes toward nature
   Orwell's view of technology
   Biographical commentary on Orwell's views
   Letters, essays, journals showing Orwell's views of nature and human liberty

Working Thesis:
Excessive media coverage influenced the outcome of the Leopold and Loeb case.

   Sources needed:
   Background/summary of Leopold & Loeb case
   Biographical information of principal figures in Leopold and Loeb case
   Description of press in Chicago in 1920s
   Actual 1924 newspaper accounts
   Assessment of effects of press on judge's decision

For a ten-page paper, you may need only one or two biographical sources, not five or six. Make sure you select enough sources for each item on your list.

Continued

2. **Collect a variety of evidence.** If you are writing a paper about the home-
    less, you may wish to balance personal accounts with statistics and expert
    opinions. A paper about *Native Son* might benefit from sources from
    African American history or accounts of contemporary race relations in ad-
    dition to critical studies of the book and biographies of Richard Wright.

3. **Avoid collecting needless or repetitive data.** The Internet has made it
    possible to access thousands of documents. Although it is important to
    grasp the sweep and range of material about your subject, avoid printing
    more items than you need for your paper.

    -   Select the most useful sources, briefly noting similar articles for con-
        firmation.
    -   Refer to the assignment and your working thesis to keep your re-
        search focused.
    -   Skim books and long documents by examining tables of contents
        and indexes to measure their usefulness before checking them out.

4. **Select reliable sources.** Recognized publishers, magazines, and estab-
    lished databases such as MLA, West Law, and Psychological Abstracts
    are edited by professionals who follow established standards. Articles
    appearing in the *New England Journal of Medicine*, the *Harvard Law
    Review*, or *Nursing* have been reviewed by physicians, attorneys, and
    nurses. On the other hand, small presses and individual websites may
    produce material based solely on rumor, anecdotal observation, and
    facts taken out of context. Do not assume that all the books in the
    library or sites found on the Internet are of equal value.

    -   Books can be evaluated by checking reviews, many of which are
        available online. You can also examine the author's use of sources.
        Does the book include a bibliography? Does the author provide
        endnotes and support his or her conclusions with facts, quotations,
        or statistics? Is the author's biography available in *Who's Who* or other
        databases? Does the author seem biased?
    -   You can get a sense of the quality of a magazine by reviewing other
        issues and examining the editorial staff. Determine the audience for
        the magazine. Publications designed for general readers like *Reader's
        Digest* or *People* will have a different purpose and tone than profes-
        sional journals in law or medicine.
    -   Verify information you find on the Web by seeking confirming arti-
        cles on established databases. Examine the author or publisher of
        the Web site. Is it a professional organization, university, or govern-
        ment agency? Or is it a small, amateur, or personal site? Does the in-
        formation seem biased or objective?

Continued

5. **Verify controversial conclusions.** A book or website might offer a striking piece of evidence or make a dramatic conclusion. Before using this material, consider the source. Was the book published by a recognized publisher? Did the article come from a biased publication? Did you find this website using an established database like InfoTrac or Medline or by searching the Web with a general search engine like Yahoo! or AltaVista?

   - Review other books, articles, or material presented by this source.
   - Read a periodical's editorial page for signs of obvious bias. Even the tone of a publication's advertising can indicate whether the source is biased or objective.
   - Select keywords from the material and search established databases for confirmation.
   - Ask a reference librarian or your instructor to assist you in evaluating sources.

6. **Distinguish between fact and opinion.** In evaluating sources it is important to separate factual data from interpretation and analysis. The author of a book, magazine article, or website might accurately report a change in oil prices but present a highly personal and subjective interpretation or prediction.

7. **Examine sources for lapses in critical thinking.** Remember that all the books, articles, and studies you discover were created by human beings who, despite their degrees or expertise, may be biased or mistaken.

   - Do not assume that everything you read is accurate or true.
   - Facts may be misrepresented, conclusions misguided, and alternative interpretations ignored.

EVALUATING ONLINE SOURCES CHECKLIST

As you gather material from sources, consider these points:

✔ **Authorship:** Does the site mention the author or webmaster? This information is often noted at the bottom of the site's home page, but does not always appear on internal pages. Does the author or webmaster include his or her e-mail address? An e-mail to the author or webmaster might yield valuable insights.

Continued

✔ **Credibility:** If you are able to identify the site's author, can you also determine if he or she has significant knowledge about the topic? Does the site have a scholarly basis, or does it merely provide someone's personal opinion? Has it been updated recently?

✔ **Objectivity:** Does a reputable organization sponsor the site? Is this organization likely to be impartial in its examination of the information? Does the organization stand to gain from persuading you to accept its position? Do you detect inflammatory language that reveals bias or prejudice?

✔ **Purpose:** Can you determine the site's intended purposes? Is the site designed to present all available evidence? Does it seem to take a side? Is the site intended to inform readers or to sell a product or service?

✔ **Audience:** Are readers expected to have an opinion prior to visiting the site? Are readers encouraged to form an opinion based solely on the information presented? Or is further investigation invited via links to related sites?

✔ **Language:** Is the information presented in a manner that allows virtually any reader to understand it? Is specialized jargon included? Does its presence have a negative effect on the presentation or the general reader's comprehension?

✔ **Presentation:** Has the site been planned and designed well? Is it easy to navigate? Are the links active, current, and relevant? Does the text reflect that careful planning has been devoted to it, including thorough proofreading? But don't allow impressive graphics, sound, and video to substitute for accuracy in the information.

✔ **Critical Thinking:** Do you detect errors in critical thinking such as hasty generalizations, dependence on anecdotal evidence, faulty comparisons, false authorities, or attacking personalities?

STRATEGIES FOR OVERCOMING PROBLEMS WITH RESEARCH

Students frequently encounter common problems in conducting library research.

1. **There are no sources on the topic.** If your library and Internet search fails to yield sufficient results, review the subject and search words you are using.

    - Check the spelling of your keywords. Failing to enter words and numbers correctly will thwart an Internet or database search.
    - Check a thesaurus for synonyms.
    - Review the Library of Congress Subject Headings for alternative search terms.
    - Review textbooks, encyclopedias, and other reference sources for search terms.
    - Ask a reference librarian or your instructor for suggestions.

2. **There are sources about the subject but none are related to your specific topic or working thesis.** If you are analyzing the role of the mother in *Death of a Salesman*, you may find numerous articles on the play or Willy Loman but nothing on his wife. You do not have to find articles that exactly match your topic or thesis. Since one of the goals of a research paper is originality, your thesis may address unexplored territory. You can still use related or background sources. Biographies of Arthur Miller might yield insights into the attitudes represented by Linda Loman. Critical commentaries may provide views about the Loman family that relate to Linda's role in the play.

    - Pointing out the lack of sources can be crucial in demonstrating the value of your paper and the uniqueness of your approach.

3. **Sources present conflicting findings or opinions.** Experts often disagree. Biographers and historians evaluate people and events differently. Scientists dispute theories and present different interpretations of data. Economists argue whether tax cuts would stimulate or slow the economy.

    - As a student you are not expected to resolve conflicts among experts, but you should report what you find.
    - On the basis of your evaluation of the evidence, you may side with one group or alter your thesis to conclude that at present it is impossible to make a definitive statement.

Continued

4. **There are several books and articles, but they present the same information or refer to a common original source.** If you discover that the five books you have selected about teenage suicide or a person's life present virtually the same material, select the most representative, relevant, or best-written book.

- Although you may select only a single source, it is important to comment on the consistency of expert opinion.

5. **The only available sources are fragmentary, biased, outdated, inaccurate, or unprofessional.** In some instances the only available sources will lack substance or quality. A controversial historical incident may have produced a rash of inflammatory editorials, biased newspaper accounts, or subjective memoirs by adversaries.

- Ask your instructor if you should consider changing your topic.
- Consult a reference librarian for alternative sources.
- As a researcher you are not responsible for the lack of evidence or the quality of sources you can locate—but you should comment on the limited value of existing evidence.

TAKING NOTES

Traditional textbooks suggest that you record notes on index cards. By placing a single fact or quotation on a single card, you can easily shuffle and reorder them when you develop an outline. However, most students now photocopy or print pages and highlight selected passages. Others will scan text directly onto a computer disk. Yet another option is to download and save full-text articles from databases. Then you may minimize photocopying costs and conserve paper by printing hard copies of only the sections you consider necessary. Better yet, you can save money and trees by highlighting (in bold or an alternate color) useful passages in the file (so they are visible on the computer monitor) for later reference in your research paper.

Whatever method you use to record information from outside sources, it is essential to accomplish three tasks:

1. **Accurately record information you will need to cite the source.**
   Books: author's full name, full title of book (including any subtitle), publisher, place of publication, and year.

- If a publisher lists several cities, choose the first location listed.
- Note editions, translators, editors, or forewords.

Articles: author's full name, full title of article (including any subtitle), full title of the magazine or newspaper, edition, volume, pages, and date.
Motion pictures: title, director, studio, city, year of release.
Videotape: title, director, production company, city, date of production or original broadcast.
Electronic sources: author's (or editor's) full name, title of website or document, sponsoring organization, date of last update, date you accessed the source, the exact Internet address.

- If you photocopy pages from a book or magazine, write the information directly on the copies for future reference.
- When printing out websites, make sure that the address appears on the printed version. If not, record the information on your printout.

2. **Double-check your notes for accuracy.** If you take notes rather than photocopy a source, make sure that you have properly copied facts, numbers, and names. Always include the page number. Understand the difference between quoting and paraphrasing sources:

Original text:

When Robert Moses began building playgrounds in New York City, there were 119. When he stopped, there were 777. Under his direction, an army of men that at times during the Depression included 84,000 laborers reshaped every park in the city and then filled the parks with zoos and skating rinks, boathouses and tennis houses, bridle paths and golf courses, 288 tennis courts and 673 baseball diamonds.

Robert A. Caro, *The Power Broker*

Student notecard: full direct quotation

Robert A. Caro, <u>The Power Broker</u>. New York: Vintage, 1975
"When Robert Moses began building playgrounds in New York City, there were 119. When he stopped, there were 777. Under his direction, an army of men that at times during the Depression included 84,000 laborers reshaped every park in the city and then filled the parks with zoos and skating rinks, boathouses and tennis houses, bridle paths and golf courses, 288 tennis courts and 673 baseball diamonds." Pg. 7

Student notecard: partial direct quotation using ellipsis (. . .) to show omitted text

---

Robert A. Caro, <u>The Power Broker</u>. New York: Vintage, 1975
"When Robert Moses began building playgrounds in New York
City, there were 119. When he stopped, there were 777. Under
his direction, an army of men . . . reshaped every park in the
city. . . ." Pg. 7

- In deleting details, make sure that your notes accurately reflect the meaning of the original text. Do not take quotations out of context that alter the author's point of view.

Student notecard: Paraphrase, putting text into your own words

---

Robert A. Caro, <u>The Power Broker</u>. New York: Vintage, 1975
Robert Moses increased the number of New York City playgrounds from 119 to 777. During the Depression as many as
80,000 workers restored every city park, embellishing them
with zoos, playgrounds, and hundreds of tennis courts and
baseball diamonds. Pg. 7

Even though the student is not copying Robert Caro word for word, he or she will have to cite Caro in the research paper to acknowledge the source of the statistics.

3. **Label research materials.**
   - Make sure that you print or photocopy all the material needed. To save paper, some library printers do not automatically print the last page of an article. Make sure your copies are complete.
   - Clip or staple articles to prevent pages from becoming mixed up.
   - Label, number, or letter your sources for easy reference. You may find it useful to write notecards for some or all of your sources so they can be easily arranged on your desk.

4. **Organize database files.**

- Consolidate files you've downloaded from databases and make a back-up disk.
- As a quick and easy reference, consolidate abstracts of the articles to form a single file that provides an overview of the items you've identified as potentially useful.

RESEARCH CHECKLIST

As you conduct your research, consider these questions:

✔ Do you fully understand the needs of the assignment? Do you know what your instructor expects in terms of topic, content, sources, and documentation?

✔ Have you narrowed your topic sufficiently to target a search for sources?

✔ Has your preliminary research given you a global view of the field? Can you detect trends or patterns in the research, prevailing theories, or conflicts?

✔ Have you developed a flexible working thesis to guide your research?

✔ Have you explored database and online sources as well as books and print articles?

✔ Are you keeping the final paper in mind as you conduct research? If you sense your paper expanding beyond its target length, narrow your topic.

✔ Does the material you select accurately and fairly represent the wider spectrum of research material, or are you taking material out of context to support a preconceived thesis?

✔ Are you recording the data needed to document your sources in the final paper?

If you have difficulties locating material, ask your instructor or reference librarian for assistance.

E-WRITING: Exploring Research Sources Online

You can use the Internet to understand more about conducting research.

1. Using a search engine like Alta Vista, Yahoo, or Google enter terms such as "conducting research," "using library sources," "evaluating Internet sources," and "locating library sources."

2. Search the Internet for online library catalogs. Simply by entering names such as "Chicago Public Library" or "Harvard University" may lead you to an online catalog.

3. Analyze your college's online library catalog. Search for a specific book or magazines location. Use the Subject search to locate information on topics you have discussed in some of your courses. What links does your college library offer? What other sources are available for future research assignments?

InfoTrac® College Edition

For additional resources go to InfoTrac College Edition, your online research library, at http://infotrac.thomsonlearning.com.

1. Select a topic you have recently discussed in one of your courses and enter it as a search term. Study the subdivisions and locate a range of articles that provide additional information about this topic.

2. Enter the name of your hometown, employer, or college as a search term to locate current articles.

Writing the Research Paper

A good research paper is actually the result or
culmination of many rough drafts.
Jeanette A. Woodward

WHAT IS A RESEARCH PAPER?

The research paper is the standard method of demonstrating your skills in many college courses. Collecting data, assembling quotations, finding evidence, and developing a thesis are essential to laying the groundwork for your paper. But before you plunge into working with sources and making citations, it is important to take three preliminary steps:

1. **Review the needs of the assignment.** If you have not examined the instructor's requirements recently, refresh your memory. Study any handouts or notes you may have made.

    *   Do you fully understand what is expected in terms of topic, content, sources, and format? If you are unsure, talk with your instructor.
    *   Do your working thesis, sources, and notes fit the scope of the assignment? Should some sources be discarded? Should other avenues of research be pursued?

2. **Take a global look at your sources and notes.** Review the full scope of what your research has revealed. Consider the whole body of evidence you have discovered, including those items you examined but did not select.

    *   What have you learned about the subject? Have you uncovered information that leads you to further narrow your topic or refine the thesis?
    *   Do sources contradict or disprove your assumptions? Should you rethink your point of view?
    *   What do the sources reveal about the state of knowledge about your topic? Is there consensus or conflict? Are there patterns in the evidence?
    *   How reliable are the sources? Are they based on a careful reading of the subject, thorough research, and controlled experiments, or are they biased and /or do they rely on anecdotal data?

- Are there sources that can be grouped together, such as articles by experts who share the same opinion or similar statistics? Can some sources be considered duplicates?
- Can you prioritize sources? Which are the most important?
- How can critical thinking help you analyze the value of what you have located?

3. **Reshape your paper by reviewing your topic, examining the evidence, and refining the working thesis.**

REFINE YOUR THESIS AND DEVELOP AN OUTLINE

After examining your sources, refine the thesis. You may have limited the original topic and need to develop a thesis that addresses the new focus of your paper. In writing shorter papers, you may have needed only a brief plan or list of ideas to guide the first draft. But in writing a research paper, it is useful to develop a full outline to organize your ideas and sources.

Working Thesis

Orwell considered contact with nature essential to individual liberty.

Revised Thesis

Winston Smith's humanity and individual autonomy are stunted not only by the brutality of Oceania and the ever-present Thought Police, but by his lack of contact with nature.

Working Outline

A working outline is a rough guide to direct your first draft. Because it is not likely to be read by anyone other than yourself, it does not have to follow any particular format. Use it as a blueprint to organize your main points and sources.

I Intro—Conventional readings of *1984*

    A Simes quote

    B Wolzheck quote

    C Janeson quote

    D Goodman quote

II Transition/Thesis—Important Role of Nature Overlooked

III Unnatural/Artificial Life in Oceania

    A "Golden Country Dream" quote (<u>1984</u> p. 29)

    B Smith and Julia in nature

    C Nature and sexual passion—(<u>1984</u> quote p. 105)

IV Nature as Orwell's Moral Gold Standard

    A Sandison quote

    B Letter to Henry Miller quote (<u>Collected Essays</u> 4:80)

V Orwell's Lack of Faith in Technology

    A Electricity quote (<u>Road</u> p. 84)

    B Bugs quote (<u>Road</u> p. 71)

VI Orwell's Doubts about Progress

    A Pleasure Spots quote (<u>Collected Essays</u> 4:80)

    B Radio quote (<u>Collected Essays</u> 4:80)

VII Conclusion

    A Sandison quote (p. 10)

    B Final Point—<u>1984</u> relevant for 21st century

Along with an outline, develop a time line to chart your progress. Make sure you budget enough time for each stage of the writing process, including revising and editing.

STRATEGIES FOR DEVELOPING AN OUTLINE

1. **Write a clear thesis statement.** The thesis is the mission statement of your paper. It should provide a clear focus for the paper and direct your first draft.

   - Use the thesis statement as a guide for selecting outside sources.

2. **Write an outline in light of your thesis and the needs of the assignment.** Make sure that your outline addresses the goals of the paper and the instructor's requirements.

Continued

3. **Don't expect that your sources will neatly fall into place like pieces of a puzzle.** In many instances, the evidence you find may be fragmentary and lead in different directions. Outline your ideas and observations, weaving into the text those sources that confirm your point of view.

4. **Use sources to support your views; don't simply summarize them.** An outline forms a skeleton or framework for the first draft. Indicate where you will place source material such as quotations, facts, or statistics.

    •   Do not feel obligated to include all the sources you have located.

5. **When writing an outline, leave ample space for alterations.**

6. **Label your sources for easy reference.** You may wish to develop a shorthand reference for each source, labeling sources A, B, C or giving them descriptive names to guide your outline.

7. **Separate longer sources for use in multiple places.** If you have located a long quotation, do not feel obligated to place it in a single block of text. Instead, you may select two or three sections and distribute them throughout the paper.

    •   When separating longer passages, make sure you do not distort the source's meaning by taking ideas out of context.

8. **Design an introduction that announces the topic, sets up the thesis, and prepares readers for the direction of the paper.** Because research papers can be long and complex, it is important to give readers a road map, an explanation of what will follow.

    •   An introduction can present the thesis, provide a rationale for the methods of research, or comment on the nature of sources. Your introduction might explain that you will compare two writers, use public opinion polls to track attitudes on race, or limit the discussion of Nixon's presidency to his domestic policies.

    •   Introductions can be used to address research problems, commenting on the lack of reliable data or conflicting opinions. Introductions can also include a justification of your approach that anticipates reader objections.

    •   As with writing any paper, you will probably come up with new ideas while writing the draft. After revising the body, you may wish to rewrite the opening and closing.

Continued

9. **Organize the body by using the modes of organization.** Clear structure plays an important role in making your paper readable and convincing. Without a clear pattern of organization, your paper may become a confusing list of quotations and statistics.

   • Use modes, such as *comparison* and *division*, to organize evidence.
   • Use transitional statements and paragraph breaks to signal changes in direction.

10. **Craft a conclusion that ends the paper on a strong point rather than a simple summary of points.** Although it may be useful to review critical points at the end of a long paper, the conclusion should leave the reader with a memorable fact, quotation, or restatement of the thesis.

WRITING THE RESEARCH PAPER

Your goal in writing the first draft, as with any paper, is to get your ideas on paper. Using outside sources, however, complicates the writing process. Students often make common errors in approaching the evidence they have collected.

STRATEGIES FOR USING SOURCES

1. **Avoid simply reporting on what you found.** The quotations, facts, and statistics you have selected should support your point of view. Avoid what some writers call the "string of pearls" effect of simply patching together outside sources with little original commentary or analysis:

   When it first opened on Broadway, *Death of a Salesman* had a great impact on audiences (Stein, 19). According to Sally Lyman, "The play captured the hidden anxiety coursing through postwar America" (17). Another critic, Timothy Baldwin, stated, "This play made the audience face its greatest fear—growing old" (98). Fred Carlson said that he walked out of the theater shaken and deeply moved (23).

   • Although outside sources may be interesting and worth quoting or paraphrasing, *your* ideas, interpretations, and arguments should form the basis of the paper.

Continued

2. **Explain any lack of sources.** If you select a new, unknown, or uncommon subject, there may be few sources directly supporting your thesis. Although readers might be impressed by your argument, they may question why you have not supported your ideas with evidence. An instructor may question if you thoroughly researched your topic. Commenting on the lack of sources can both demonstrate the uniqueness of your approach and justify the lack of outside sources:

   Critics of *Death of a Salesman* have concentrated on the male characters, examining Willy Loman's dreams, his relationship to Biff, his sons' conflicts. Of 125 articles published in the last four years about this play, none focus on the essential role of Linda Loman, who serves as the axis for the male conflicts in the play.

3. **Summarize conflicting opinions.** One of the responsibilities of a researcher is to fairly represent the available body of evidence. If respected authorities disagree, you should explain the nature of the controversy:

   Scientists debate whether this disorder is hereditary. Yale researchers Brown and Smith cite the British twin study as evidence of a genetic link (35–41). However, both the American Medical Association and the National Institutes of Health insist the small numbers of subjects in the twin study do not provide sufficient evidence to support any conclusions (Kendrick 19–24).

4. **Indicate if sources represent widely held views.** Often you will find that sources present similar views or interpretations. If you find four or five sources that present the same information, you may wish to select the source that is the most thorough, most recent, or best written. You can emphasize the significance of this source by mentioning that its ideas are shared by others:

   Nearly all experts on teenage suicide support Jane Diaz's observation that low self-esteem, stress, and substance abuse are the principal contributing factors to the current rise in adolescent suicide (Smith 28; Johnson 10–15; King 89–92).

5. **Comment on the quality as well as quantity of your sources.** Not all sources have equivalent value. Sources may be inaccurate, biased, or based on limited evidence. If you conduct research on controversial issues or events, you may find little reliable material. If you are unable to

Continued

determine which source is closest to the truth or which study is accurate, inform your readers of the dilemma you face:

Although the 1908 railroad strike received national attention, few major newspapers offered more than superficial reports. Sensational accounts of lynching, rape, and murder appeared in New York and Chicago tabloids. The radical *Torch of Labor* blamed the deaths of two strikers on a plot engineered by Wall Street bankers. The conservative *Daily World* insisted union organizers were bent on overthrowing the government. Most sources, however, do agree that Red Williams played a critical role in organizing a labor protest that ultimately weakened the emerging Transport Workers Union.

GUIDELINES FOR USING DIRECT QUOTATIONS

Direct quotations give power and authority to your research paper by introducing the words of others just as they were written or stated. But to be effective, direct quotations have to be carefully chosen, accurately presented, and skillfully woven into the text of your paper.

1. **Limit use of direct quotations.** Avoid reproducing long blocks of text, unless direct evidence is essential for accuracy or emphasis. In many instances, you can summarize and paraphrase information.

   - Use direct quotes when they are brief, memorable, and so well stated that a paraphrase would reduce their impact. Avoid using direct quotes when you can accurately restate the information in a documented paraphrase.
   - **Remember, the focus of a research paper is *your* ideas, observations, and conclusions, not a collection of direct quotations.**

2. **Link direct quotations into your commentary.** Avoid isolating quotations:

   Faulty:
   Television advertising exploded in the Fifties. "Advertising agencies increased spending on television commercials from $10 million in 1948 to $2 billion in 1952" (Smith 16). These revenues financed the rapid development of a new industry.

   Revised:
   Television advertising exploded in the Fifties. According to Kai Smith, "Advertising agencies increased spending on television commercials

from $10 million in 1948 to $2 billion in 1952" (16). These revenues financed the rapid development of a new industry.

Or

Television advertising exploded in the Fifties, with advertising agencies increasing spending "from $10 million in 1948 to $2 billion in 1952" (Smith 16). These revenues financed the rapid development of a new industry.

3. **Introduce block quotes with a complete sentence followed by colon:** The Quiz Show Scandal of the 1950s shook public confidence in the new medium. The idea that the highly-popular shows were rigged to ensure ratings infuriated and disillusioned the public:

> NBC received thousands of letters and telephone calls from irate viewers who felt cheated. Although the public readily accepted that Westerns and soap operas were fictional, they believed that the teachers and housewives who appeared on shows like "Twenty-One" were "real people" like themselves. Having followed their favorite contestants week after week, loyal viewers strongly identified with people they considered genuine. Learning that all the furrowed brows and lipbiting were choreographed, they felt duped. (Brown 23)

4. **Provide background information to establish the value of direct quotations.** Bibliographical entries at the end of your paper may explain a source but do not help readers understand its significance:

Faulty:
President Roosevelt showed signs of declining health as early as 1942. Sheridan noted, "His hands trembled when writing, he complained of headaches, and he often seemed unable to follow the flow of conversation around him" (34–35).

Revised:
President Roosevelt showed signs of declining health as early as 1942. George Sheridan, a young naval aide who briefed the White House during the Battle of Midway, was shocked by the President's condition. Sheridan noted, "His hands trembled when writing, he complained of headaches, and he often seemed unable to follow the flow of conversation around him" (34–35).

5. **Indicate quotations within quotations.** Although most writers try to avoid using direct quotations that appear in another source, sometimes it cannot be avoided. You can easily indicate a quote within a quote with (qtd. in):

Original Source

From Sandra Bert's *The Plague* (page 23)

The medical community of San Francisco was overwhelmed by the sudden increase in AIDS cases in the early 1980s. Tim Watson, a resident at the time, said, "It was like being hit by a tidal wave. We went home every night absolutely stunned by the influx of dying young men."

Research Paper quoting Tim Watson:

Within a few years the number of AIDS cases, especially in the Bay Area, exploded. Physicians were shocked by the influx of patients with untreatable infections. "It was like being hit by a tidal wave," Watson remembered (qtd. in Bert, 23).

6. **Accurately delete unneeded material from quotations.** You can abbreviate long quotations, deleting irrelevant or unimportant details by using ellipsis points (. . .). Three evenly spaced periods indicate words have been deleted from a direct quotation:

Original:

The governor vetoed the education bill, which had been backed by a coalition of taxpayers and unions, because it cut aid to inner city schools.

—James Kirkland

Shortened quotation using ellipsis points:

Kirkland reported that "the governor vetoed the education bill . . . because it cut aid to inner city schools."

- Use a period and three ellipsis points (four dots. . . .) to indicate deletion of one or more full sentences.
- Avoid making deletions that distort the original meaning. Do not eliminate qualifying statements:

Original:

Given the gang wars, the failure of treatment programs, the rising number of addicts, I regretfully think we should legalize drugs until we can find better solutions to the problem.

—Mayor Wells

Improper use of ellipsis points:

At a recent press conference, Mayor Wells stated, "I . . . think we should legalize drugs . . ."

7. **Use brackets to insert words or indicate alterations.** In some instances, you may have to insert a word to prevent confusion or a grammatical error.

Original:
> George Roosevelt [no relation to the President] left the Democratic Party in 1935, troubled by the deepening Depression. Roosevelt considered the New Deal a total failure.
> —Nancy Stewart

Brackets enclose inserted word to prevent confusion:
> As the Depression deepened, many deserted the Democratic Party, seeking more radical solutions to the worsening economy. According to Stewart, "[George] Roosevelt considered the New Deal a total failure."

Original:
> Poe, Whitman, and Ginsburg are among some of America's greatest poets.
> —John Demmer

Brackets enclose altered verb:
> Demmer states that "Poe . . . [is] among some of America's greatest poets."

STRATEGIES FOR CITING SOURCES

Many students find citing sources one of the challenging aspects of writing a research paper. Mastering the details of accounting for each source can be frustrating. It is important to understand that documenting where you obtained information for your paper serves three key purposes:

1. **Citations prevent allegations of plagiarism.** Plagiarism occurs when you present the facts, words, or ideas of someone else as your own. Students often find it difficult to believe that copying something out of *The World Book* for a term paper can be considered a crime, but plagiarism has serious consequences. In many colleges students who submit a plagiarized paper will automatically fail the course. In some schools, students will be expelled. Outside of academics, plagiarism (often called "copyright infringement") has ruined the careers of politicians, artists, and executives. Prominent columnists and writers have been fired from newspapers and magazines for using the ideas of others without acknowledging their original source. Hollywood studios have been sued by artists who claim ideas from their rejected screenplays were used in other films.

   - Accurate documentation protects you from plagiarism by clearly labeling borrowed ideas.

Continued

2. **Citations support your thesis.** Attorneys arguing a case before a judge or jury present labeled exhibits to prove their theory of a case. As a researcher, you support your thesis by introducing expert testimony, facts, case histories, and eyewitness accounts. Like an attorney, you have to clearly identify the source for evidence for it to be credible. A paper about crime that draws upon statistics from the FBI and studies from the Justice Department will be more credible than one relying only on personal observations and opinions.

   • The more controversial your thesis, the more readers will demand supporting evidence.

3. **Citations refer readers to other sources.** Citations not only illustrate which ideas originated with the writer and which were drawn from other sources, but they also alert readers to where they can find more information. Through your citations, readers may learn of a biography or a Web site offering additional evidence.

Exceptions to Citing Sources

You do not need to use citations for every fact, quotation, or idea you present in your paper:

1. **Common expressions or famous quotations.** Famous sayings by people such as Shakespeare, Jesus, or Benjamin Franklin (for example, "To err is human" or "I am the resurrection") do not have to be cited, even when presented as direct quotes. If you are unsure, ask your instructor.

2. **Facts considered in the "realm of common knowledge."** You do not have to provide a citation if you referred to a source to check a fact that is readily available in numerous sources. You do not have to cite *The Encyclopedia Britannica* if you used it to find out where Arthur Miller was born or when North Dakota became a state. No one will accuse you of stealing facts that are commonly known and not subject to change or interpretation.

In almost every other instance, however, you have to acknowledge the use of outside material:

1. **Direct quotations.** Whenever you quote a source word for word, you must place it in quotation marks and cite its source.

2. **Indirect quotations or paraphrases.** Even if you do not copy a source, but state the author's ideas in your own words, you must cite the source. Changing a few words or condensing a page of text into a few sentences does not alter the fact that you are using someone else's ideas.

3. **Specific facts, statistics, and numbers.** Data will be credible and acceptable only if you present the source. If you state, "Last year 54,450 drunk drivers were arrested in California," readers will naturally wonder where you obtained that number. Statistics make credible evidence only if readers trust their source.

4. **Graphs, charts, and other visual aids.** Indicate the source of any graphic you reproduce.

   - You must also cite the source for information you use to create a visual display.

STRATEGIES FOR REVISING AND EDITING RESEARCH PAPERS

1. **Review the assignment, thesis, and working outline.**

2. **Examine your draft for use of sources.**

   - Does the draft fulfill the needs of the assignment?
   - Does the text support the thesis?
   - Is the thesis properly placed? Should it appear in the opening or the conclusion?
   - Are enough sources presented?
   - Is there any evidence that should be included or deleted?
   - Do you provide enough original commentary, or is your paper merely a collection of facts and quotes?

3. **Read the draft aloud.**

   - Does the paper have an even style and tone? Are there awkward transitions between sources and your commentary?

4. **Revise the introduction and conclusion.**

5. **Edit for mechanical and spelling errors. Make sure your paper follows the appropriate style for documenting sources.**

DOCUMENTATION STYLES

Writers document their use of outside sources with one of several methods. The MLA and APA formats are commonly used in the humanities and social sciences. Both methods provide guidelines for placing parenthetical notes after quoting or paraphrasing outside sources and listing them at the end of the paper. Traditional textbooks suggest recording each source on a note card so they can be easily shuffled and placed in alphabetical order. If you are writing on a computer, you may find it easier to scroll down and enter each source as you refer to it.

THE MLA STYLE

The MLA style, created by the Modern Language Association, is used in language and literature courses. Parenthetical notes listing the author or title and page numbers are inserted after quotations and paraphrases. At the end of the paper all the sources are alphabetized on a "Works Cited" page. For full details about using the MLA style, consult Joseph Gibaldi's *MLA Style Manual and Guide to Scholarly Publishing*, second edition, or *MLA Handbook for Writers of Research Papers*, sixth edition.

STRATEGIES FOR WRITING PARENTHETICAL NOTES

Parenthetical notes usually include an author's last name and a page number. If no author is listed, titles—sometimes abbreviated—are used. To keep the notes as brief as possible, the MLA format does not precede page numbers with *p.*, *pp.*, or commas. The parenthetical note is considered part of the sentence and comes before the final mark of punctuation. Notes should be placed as close to the source as possible without interrupting the flow of the text.

1. **Parenthetical notes include author and page number.** A direct quotation from Ralph Ellison's novel *Invisible Man* is indicated with a parenthetical note placed after it:

    The novel's unnamed character calls himself invisible because society does not recognize him as a human being. He defends his

    Continued

retreat from society, realizing that many would view his decision as a sign of irresponsibility. "Responsibility," he argues, "rests on recognition, and recognition is a form of agreement" (Ellison 14).

2. **Parenthetical notes include only page numbers if the author is clearly identified in the text:**

Sheila Smitherin praised Ellison's novel, stating that modern black literature "was born on the pages of *Invisible Man*" (32).

3. **If two or more sources are cited within a sentence, notes are inserted after the material that is quoted or paraphrased:**

Smith stated that the novel "exposed the deep-rooted racism society was unwilling to confront" (34), leading one columnist to argue that the book should be taught in every high school (Wilson 12–13).

4. **Long quotations are indented ten spaces without quotation marks:**

The Group Theater revolutionized American drama. According to Frank Kozol, the members tried to create something then unseen on the New York stage:

> Clurman and his followers wanted to create a new kind of theater. They not only wanted to produce new, socially relevant plays, but create a new relationship between playwright and cast. It would be a collective effort. Designed to be a theater without stars, actors lived together and shared living expenses. They were infused with the revolutionary spirit of the times. The Group Theater soon launched the career of Clifford Odets, whose plays were among the most poignant depictions of life during the Great Depression. (Taylor 34–35)

Notice that the parenthetical note appears outside the final punctuation of the last sentence.

STRATEGIES FOR WRITING
A WORKS CITED PAGE

List all sources you have cited on a separate sheet at the end of your paper, titled "Works Cited." If you include works you have read for background but not actually cited, title the page "Works Consulted."

- Arrange the list of works alphabetically by the author's last name or first significant word of the title if no author is listed:

    Jones, Wilson. Chicago Today. New York: Putnam, 2002.
    "A New Look for Toronto." Toronto Magazine Fall 2003: 21.

- For sources with more than one author, alphabetize by the first author's last name:

    Zinter, Mary, and Jan Ames. First Aid. New York: Dial, 2002.

- Begin each citation even with the left margin, and indent subsequent lines five spaces. Double-space the entire page. Do not separate entries with additional spaces:

    Abrams, Jane. "Rebuilding America's Cities." Plain Dealer [Cleveland] 21 Jan. 2002: A11.
    Brown, Gerald. The Death of the Central City: The Malling of America. New York: Macmillan, 2003.

- If more than one source is used for an author, alphabetize the works but list the author's last name only once, substituting three hyphens for the name in subsequent citations:

    Keller, Joseph. Assessing Blame. New York: Columbia UP, 2003.
    ---. Quality Control. New York: Miller, 2000.

GUIDELINES FOR LISTING SOURCES IN WORKS CITED AND PARENTHETICAL NOTES

Books

1. Write the author's last name, first name, then any initial. Copy the name as written on the title page. "C. W. Brown" would appear as:

    Brown, C. W.

    Omit any degrees or titles such as Ph.D. or Dr.

2. State the full title of the book. Place a colon between the main heading and any subtitle. Underline all the words and punctuation in the title, except for the final period.

    Brown, C. W. <u>Sharks and Lambs: Wall Street in the Nineties</u>.

3. Record the city of publication, publisher, and date of publication. If the book lists several cities, use only the first. If the city is outside the United States, add an abbreviation for the country. If an American city may be unfamiliar, you can include an abbreviation for the state. Record the main words of the publisher, deleting words like "publishing" or "press" (Monroe for Monroe Publishing Company). Use the initials "UP" for "University Press." End the citation with the last year of publication.

WORKS CITED ENTRY FOR BOOK WITH ONE AUTHOR:

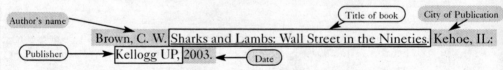

Brown, C. W. Sharks and Lambs: Wall Street in the Nineties. Kehoe, IL: Kellogg UP, 2003.

PARENTHETICAL NOTE:
  (Brown 12)

Book with Two or Three Authors

WORKS CITED ENTRY:
  Smith, David, John Adams, and Chris Cook. <u>Writing On-line</u>. New York: Macmillan, 2000.

PARENTHETICAL NOTE:
  (Smith, Adams, and Cook 23–24)

Books with Four or More Authors

WORKS CITED ENTRY:
Chavez, Nancy, et al. <u>Mexico Today</u>. New York: Putnam, 2003.

PARENTHETICAL NOTE:
(Chavez et al. 87)

Book with Corporate Author

WORKS CITED ENTRY:
National Broadcasting Company. <u>Programming Standards</u>. New York: National Broadcasting Company, 2002.

PARENTHETICAL NOTE:
(National Broadcasting Company 112)

To avoid a cumbersome parenthetical note, you can mention the author or title in the text:

According to the National Broadcasting Company's <u>Programming Standards</u>, "No single executive should be able to cancel a program" (214).

Book with Unnamed Authors

WORKS CITED ENTRY:
<u>New Yale Atlas.</u> New York: Random. 2003.

PARENTHETICAL NOTE:
(<u>New Yale</u> 106)

Book with Multiple Volumes

WORKS CITED ENTRY:
Eisenhower, Dwight. <u>Presidential Correspondence</u>. Vol. 2. New York: Dutton, 1960. 6 vols.

PARENTHETICAL NOTE:
(Eisenhower 77).

If you cite more than one volume in your paper, indicate the number:

(Eisenhower 2: 77)

Book in Second or Later Edition

WORKS CITED ENTRY:
Franklin, Marcia. <u>Modern France</u>. 3rd ed. Philadelphia: Comstock, 1987.

PARENTHETICAL NOTE:
(Franklin 12)

Work in an Anthology

WORKS CITED ENTRY:
Ford, John M. "Preflash." The Year's Best Fantasy. Eds. Ellen Datlow and Terri Windling. New York: St. Martin's, 1989. 265–82.
PARENTHETICAL NOTE:
(Ford 265–66)

Note: If you include more than one work from the same anthology, list the anthology in the Works Cited section separately under the editors' names and list individual entries in a shortened form:

Ford, John M. "Preflash." Datlow and Windling 265–82.

Book in Translation

WORKS CITED ENTRY:
Verne, Jules. Twenty Thousand Leagues Under the Sea. Trans. Michel Michot. Boston: Pitman, 1992.
PARENTHETICAL NOTE:
(Verne 65)

Book with Editor or Editors

WORKS CITED ENTRY:
Benson, Nancy, ed. Ten Great American Plays. New York: Columbia UP, 2002.
PARENTHETICAL NOTE:
(Benson 23)

The preceding parenthetical note would be used to cite Benson's comments.

Book with Author and Editor

WORKS CITED ENTRY:
Gissing, George. Workers in the Dawn. Ed. Jason Day. London: Oxford UP, 1982.
PARENTHETICAL NOTE:
(Gissing 78)

Book in a Series

WORKS CITED ENTRY:
Swessel, Karyn, ed. Northern Ireland Today. Modern Europe Ser. 3. New York: Wilson, 2003.
PARENTHETICAL NOTE:
(Swessel 34)

Republished Book

WORKS CITED ENTRY:
Smith, Jane. <u>The Jersey Devil</u>. 1922. New York: Warner, 2002.
PARENTHETICAL NOTE:
(Smith 23–25)

Periodicals

Newspaper Article

WORKS CITED ENTRY:

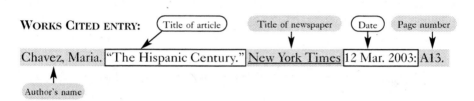

PARENTHETICAL NOTE:
(Chavez)

Note: If an article has only one page, page numbers are not included in parenthetical notes.

Magazine Article

WORKS CITED ENTRY:
Janssen, Mary. "Iran Today." <u>Time</u> 25 Mar. 2003: 34+.

Note: If an article appears on nonconsecutive pages, list the first page followed by a "+" sign.

PARENTHETICAL NOTE:
(Janssen 38)

Scholarly Article

WORKS CITED ENTRY:
Grant, Edward. "The Hollywood Ten: Fighting the Blacklist." <u>California Film Quarterly</u> 92.2
(2002): 14–32.
PARENTHETICAL NOTE:
(Grant 21–23)

Newspaper or Magazine Article with Unnamed Author

WORKS CITED ENTRY:
"The Legacy of the Gulf War." <u>American History</u> 12 Mar. 2003: 23–41.

PARENTHETICAL NOTE:
("Legacy" 25)

Letter to the Editor

WORKS CITED ENTRY:
Roper, Jack. Letter. <u>Chicago Defender</u> 12 Jan. 2002, sec. B: 12.

PARENTHETICAL NOTE:
(Roper)

Other Print Sources

Encyclopedia Article with Author

WORKS CITED ENTRY:

Author → Keller, Christopher. "Lisbon." World Book Encyclopedia. 2003.

Entry — Title of encyclopedia — Date

Note: Provide edition number if given.

PARENTHETICAL NOTE:
(Keller)

Note: Page numbers are not used with works in which articles are arranged alphabetically.

Encyclopedia Article with Unnamed Author

WORKS CITED ENTRY:
"Lisbon." <u>Columbia Illustrated Encyclopedia</u>. 2002.

PARENTHETICAL NOTE:
("Lisbon")

Pamphlet with Author

WORKS CITED ENTRY:
Tindall, Gordon. <u>Guide to New York Churches</u>. New York: Chamber of Commerce, 1998.
PARENTHETICAL NOTE:
(Tindall 76–78)

Pamphlet with Unnamed Author

WORKS CITED ENTRY:
<u>Guide to New York Museums</u>. New York: Columbia U. 2003.
PARENTHETICAL NOTE:
(<u>Guide</u> 176–82)

The Bible

WORKS CITED ENTRY:
<u>The Holy Bible: New International Version</u>. Grand Rapids: Zondervan, 1988.

Note: Titles of sacred texts are not underlined, unless they are specific editions.

PARENTHETICAL NOTE:
(Mark 2:4–9)

Nonprint Sources

Motion Picture

WORKS CITED ENTRY:

Note: You may wish to include names of performers or screenwriters if they are of special interest to readers. These names should be inserted between the title and the distributor.

Television Program

WORKS CITED ENTRY:
"The Long Goodbye." <u>Law and Order</u>. Dir. Jane Hong. Writ. Peter Wren. Perf. Rita Colletti, Diane Nezgod, and Vicki Shimi. NBC. WTMJ-4, Milwaukee. 12 May 2003.

Videotape or DVD

WORKS CITED ENTRY:
  Colonial Williamsburg. Prod. Janet Freud. Videocassette. Amer. Home Video, 1996.

Note: You may include information about the director, performers, or screenwriters if these are important for readers. These names should be inserted between the title and the distributor.

Live Performance of a Play

WORKS CITED ENTRY:
  All My Sons. By Arthur Miller. Dir. Anita Dayin. Lyric Theater, New York. 10 May 2003.

Speech

WORKS CITED ENTRY:
  Goode, Wilmont. "America in the Next Century." Chicago Press Club. 12 Oct. 2003.

Personal or Telephone Interview

WORKS CITED ENTRY:
  Weston, Thomas. Personal interview. 21 May 2003.

In the preceding citation, you would substitute "Telephone" for "Personal" if the interview was conducted by telephone.

Parenthetical Notes for Nonprint Sources

Because nonprint sources do not have page numbers and often have long titles, parenthetical notes can be cumbersome. Most writers avoid inserting citations by mentioning the source within the text:

  Multiple personality disorder was featured in a recent episode of Law and Order.

  In Gone With the Wind special effects were used to re-create the burning of Atlanta.

  Interviewed in the fall of 2003, Laura Dornan suggested that many critics failed to see the feminist theme in her play.

Electronic Sources

CD-ROM

WORKS CITED ENTRY:
"Understanding Macbeth." Master Dramas. CD-ROM. New York: Educational Media, 2002.

E-mail

WORKS CITED ENTRY:
Ballard, Morton D. "Rental Cars." E-mail to Germaine Reinhardt. 21 May 2003.

Electronic Journal

WORKS CITED ENTRY:
Smith, Perry. "Truman Capote and Kansas." Phoenix 2.7 (2003). 15 Sep. 2003 <http://www. englishlit.com/hts/phoenix/index>.

Article from Online Newspaper

WORKS CITED ENTRY:
"Long Day's Journey Into Night Production Disappointing." New York Times on the Web 17 Mar. 2003. 22 Apr. 2003 <http://www.nytimes.com/aponline/a/ ap-play.html>.

Reference Database

WORKS CITED ENTRY:
The Emerald Project: Irish Literature from 1500–2000. 2000 Boston University. 21 Oct. 2000 <http://www/bostonuniv/emerald/>.

Electronic Texts

Many books are available online. Because they lack page numbers, mention the title within the text to avoid long parenthetical notes.

WORKS CITED ENTRY:
Gissing, George. Demos. London, 1892. The Electronic Text Center. Ed. Jacob Korgman. Aug. 2002. U of Michigan Library. 5 Mar. 2003 <http//etext.lib.michigan.edu/cgibin/ browsemixed?ed5gisgeor5revolution&utopia/archive/eng>.

Web Pages

Web pages vary greatly. In general, include the name of the person or organization that created the site, the title (if there is not a title, you can use a description, such as the one used in the next entry), the date of creation or most recent update, the date of access, and the URL.

WORKS CITED ENTRY:
   Chicago Irish Center. Home page. 5 Apr. 2003. 10 May 2003 <http://www.chi.irish.cent.org>.

Discussion Group Posting

WORKS CITED ENTRY:
   Baker, Jordan.."Golf Today." Online posting. 2 Mar. 2003. Professional Sports Discussion List. 15 Mar. 2003 <http://www.prosports.com/posting/>.

Synchronous Communication

To cite a posting from forums such as MOO, MUD, or IRC, include names of speakers, a description of the event, the date, the name of the forum, date of access, and telnet address:

WORKS CITED ENTRY:
   Gladkin, Dorcas. Melville discussion of "Biblical Symbolism in Moby Dick." 19 Oct. 2000. MediaMOO. 1 Nov. 2000 <telnet://www.litcafe/homepages/smith/melville.html>.

FTP

To cite material retrieved by FTP (file transfer protocol), include the uniform resource locator, date of creation, date of access, and electronic address:

WORKS CITED ENTRY:
   "Hamlet Act I." The Electronic Shakespeare Project. Ed. Nancy Hamilton. 22 Sept. 2000. U. of Iowa. 12 Oct. 2000 <ftp://hamlet.engl.ui.edu/pub/hamlet>.

Gopher

To cite information retrieved by Gopher, include the uniform resource locator, date of creation, date of access, and electronic address:

WORKS CITED ENTRY:
   Simes, David. "Understanding Orwell's Vision." 22 Jul. 2003. 13 pp. 7 Aug. 2003 <gopher://h-net. ukw.edu/oo/orwell/internet-cit>.

Linked Sources

MLA does not provide a method of citing hypertext links, but the following format allows readers to follow your search:

WORKS CITED ENTRY:

Trainer, Lois. "F. Scott Fitzgerald." Online posting. 4 Aug. 2003. Ansaxnet. 10 Oct. 2000
<http://www.amlit/edu>. Lkd. <http://www.yalelit.edu/biography>.

SAMPLE RESEARCH PAPER USING MLA STYLE
(with Cover Page and Formal Outline)

No page
number

Title centered
one third
down from
top of page

Writer's name

Course
number,
professor's
name,
date

The Role of Nature in

Orwell's <u>1984</u>

by

Gordon Comstock

English 102

Professor Brandeis

10 May 2004

Note: If your instructor does not request a separate cover page, the first page of your paper should include the title and your name:

Comstock 1

Gordon Comstock

English 102

Professor Brandeis

10 May 2004

The Role of Nature in

Orwell's <u>1984</u>

Last name
with
lowercase
Roman
numeral
used for
outline page
numbers

Outline

Thesis statement: Winston Smith's humanity and individual autonomy are stunted not only by the brutality of Oceania and the ever-present Thought Police, but by his lack of contact with nature.

I. Most commentators view Orwell's last novel as a grim account of perverted Socialism and the abuse of technology.

II. Most readers have overlooked the role of nature in 1984. Winston Smith's lack of contact with nature robs him of his humanity.

III. Smith rebels against both the dictatorship of Big Brother and the artificiality of his environment.

    A. Smith lives in a London of shabby houses and soulless concrete towers.

    B. Food and fiber in Oceania are artificial and dehumanizing.

IV. Smith escapes this world only in dreams of a pasture he calls "The Golden Country."

    A. The dream provides a background for a sexual encounter.

    B. Winston Smith experiences a similar landscape in reality when he travels into the country with Julia.

        1. Nature provides Smith and Julia with inspiration and comfort.

        2. Smith and Julia can only enjoy sex in a natural setting, away from society.

V. Smith realizes the Party controls its citizens by separating them from reality.

VI. Nature was Orwell's "moral gold standard."

    A. Orwell did not share the Left's faith in scientific progress.

    B. Orwell sensed that even benign uses of technology designed to make life more comfortable had sinister implications.

        1. Artificial environments eliminated contact with nature.

        2. Controlled environments allowed for manipulation and deadened thought.

VII. Orwell viewed contact with nature as essential for society to be just, humane, and decent. 1984 remains relevant in the twentyfirst century of cyberspace and "virtual" realities.

Comstock 1

The Role of Nature in Orwell's 1984

Introduction

Review of
critical views
using selected
direct
quotations

Most commentators view Orwell's last novel as a grim account of perverted Socialism, a vision of a society dominated by Big Brother, a god-like Stalin figure. "Orwell was looking backward, not forward," David Simes argues, "seeing the future as a Nazi state with nuclear weapons" (16–17). Nancy Wolzheck offers the view that "Orwell saw the centralization of power as the enemy of human individuality and liberty" (192). "The principal theme of 1984," Edward Janeson writes, "is the corruption of political power" (181). Wilson Goodman asserts, "Orwell's novel reveals the horror of totalitarianism coupled with inhuman uses of technology" (18–19).

Transition

Comment on
the lack of
critical
sources on
this theme
Thesis

But most readers have overlooked a central element in 1984, the role of nature. Winston Smith's humanity and individual autonomy are stunted not only by the brutality of Oceania and the ever-present Thought Police, but by his lack of contact with nature.

Summary of
novel
focusing on
student's
thesis

Orwell's protagonist Winston Smith rebels not only against the brutal dictatorship of Big Brother but the artificiality of the world created by the Party. Smith lives in a London of shabby nineteenth-century houses and soulless concrete towers. He moves through a realm of artificial structures and windowless cubicles devoid of nature. Food and fiber in Oceania bear little resemblance to natural products; they are manufactured from synthetics. Smith survives on a diet of processed foods and imitation coffee. He only has a childhood memory of lemons, a fruit he has not seen in thirty years. Omnipresent telescreens simultaneously bombard him with propaganda and record his every move. In this artificial world, Smith's natural instincts for comfort, companionship, and freedom are demeaned and criminalized. Sex, the most natural instinct in humans, has been oppressed and sullied so that Smith's only contacts with women since his divorce have been with prostitutes.

In 1984. Smith escapes this grim world only in his sleep, when he dreams of what he calls the "Golden Country":

Block
quotation

> It was an old, rabbit-bitten pasture, with a foot track wandering across it and a mole-hole here and there. In the ragged hedge on the opposite side of the field the boughs of the elm trees were swaying

very faintly in the breeze, their leaves just stirring in the dense
masses like women's hair. (29)

This conventional bit of countryside becomes the setting for eroticism. A
dream girl runs toward Smith, tossing aside her clothes in disdainful ges-
tures "belonging to the ancient time" (29).

Smith encounters this dream landscape when he and Julia slip from
London to escape the ever-present telescreens that track their every move-
ment and prevent them from consummating their illegal relationship. Meet-
ing in the country, they enter a rabbit-bitten pasture with leaves like
"women's hair." Like the girl in the dream, Julia sheds her Junior Anti-Sex
League sash in defiance. Smith and Julia can only enjoy sexual intimacy
apart from civilization, in the wild where their passion is not blunted by social restraint. This freedom is difficult to maintain in the city, forcing them
to hole up like criminals in a dingy room to escape detection.

Nature provides Smith and Julia with inspiration and comfort, vitalizing
their sexual instincts. Nature allows them to feel that their biological urges
are wholesome and fundamental, elements linking them to the apolitical
world of flowers and birds. Smith wants to feel not "merely the love of one
person" but "the animal instinct, the simple undifferentiated desire" which
will "tear the Party to pieces" (105). Nature gives Smith the spirit to rebel,
to energize elements of humanity the Party seeks to eradicate, sully, and
trivialize.

Smith realizes that his alienation, his sense of superfluousness is caused
not only by political oppression but by his separation from nature. The Party
achieves its power not only through surveillance, censorship, and torture,
but by distorting natural law. During Smith's interrogation, O'Brien insists
that " 'the stars are bits of fire a few kilometers away. We could reach them
if we wanted to. Or we could blot them out' " (219). By altering people's con-
cept of nature, the Party assumes all power. Separated from reality, the citi-
zen of Oceania is enveloped in the artificial, managed world of the state, with
no independence.

Nature, according to Alan Sandison, was Orwell's "moral gold standard"
(10). Nature was an essential part of Orwell's judgment. Writing to Henry
Miller, whose books he admired, Orwell chided Miller for wandering off "into
a kind of reverie where the laws of ordinary reality were slipped just a little
but not too much" (Collected Essays 4:80). Orwell added, ". . . I have a sort

Selected use of direct quotations

Direct quotation of dialogue

Ellipsis indicating deleted words

of belly-to-earth attitude and always feel uneasy when I get away from the ordinary world where grass is green, stones hard etc." (4 : 80).

Orwell saw the loss of nature as the inevitable result of mechanical progress. Technology was the major tenet of the ideologies of Orwell's pre-environmentalist era. Mussolini drained the Pontine marshes; Hitler constructed the autobahn; Stalin erected huge hydroelectric dams. Orwell, unlike most Socialists of his generation, did not share the Left's faith in scientific progress. He even doubted the role of electricity, the pet project of Lenin and Stalin, in making the world better. He viewed electricity as a "queer spectacle . . . showering miracles upon people with empty bellies. . . . Twenty million people are underfed but literally everyone in England has access to a radio" (Orwell Road 84).

In The Road to Wigan Pier, Orwell decried the slums he saw in Depression-era Britain. He was also distressed by the fact that the poor were deloused before being allowed to move into new low-income housing. "Bugs are bad," he noted, "but a state of affairs in which men will allow themselves to be dipped like sheep is worse" (71).

Orwell found something insidious and dangerous even in the most benign uses of technology. Writing in 1946, he criticized the proposed development of postwar "pleasure spots" in the same way he denounced the "hygiene" in public housing. The planned resorts he read about in "slick magazines" would be comprised of artificial lagoons, heated swimming pools, sunlamps, and glass-covered tennis courts. Examining the characteristics of such artificial playlands, Orwell saw many of the same elements he would later depict in harsher terms in 1984:

1. One is never alone.
2. One never does anything for oneself.
3. One is never within sight of wild vegetation or natural objects of any kind.
4. Light and temperature are always artificially regulated.
5. One is never out of the sound of music.

(Collected Essays 4:80)

Orwell found the music to be particularly disturbing and the most important standard ingredient of the modern artificial environment:

Its function is to prevent thought and conversation, and to shut out any natural sound, such as the song of birds or the whistling of the wind, that might otherwise intrude. The radio is already consciously

---

Margin notes:

Ellipsis used to delete unnecessary details

Block quotation

Block quotation with ellipsis

used for this purpose by innumerable people. In very many English homes the radio·is literally never turned off, though it is manipulated from time to time so as to make sure that only light music will come out of it. I know people who will keep the radio playing all through a meal and at the same time continue talking just loudly enough for the voices and the music to cancel each other out. . . . The music prevents the conversation from becoming serious . . . while the chatter of voices stops one from listening attentively to the music and thus prevents the onset of that dreadful thing, thought. (<u>Collected Essays</u> 4:80)

Orwell drew on his observations of the radio in middle class English homes to envision the telescreens of Oceania.

<u>1984</u> exaggerated trends Orwell saw taking place around him. The danger to humanity was not only totalitarian governments but science and technology. The growing artificiality of life, whether inspired by tasteless commercialism or state planning, threatens human individuality and ability to make rational judgments about the world. In a natural environment all men and women are equal in their response to the world. In the artificial universe created by technology the individual can only respond to an environment created by other humans, a world designed to curtail thought, deceive, and control.

Orwell saw nature as an essential ingredient in any society that wishes to be just, humane, and decent. "Man only stays human," Orwell argued, "by preserving large patches of simplicity in his life" (<u>Collected Essays</u> 4:80). Modern inventions, though they make life easier and more comfortable under the best circumstances, can have severe consequences on the individual and "weaken his consciousness, dull his curiosity, and, in general, drive him nearer to the animals" (<u>Collected Essays</u> 4:81). As Alan Sandison notes in <u>The Last Man in Europe,</u> "the greatest moral danger Orwell can envision for a man is that he should be denied contact with the ordinary world where grass is green, stones hard" (10).

<u>1984</u> then remains a relevant novel. Orwell's vision of a Stalinist nightmare state may no longer seem compelling, but his observations about the growing artificiality of life and the need for humans to maintain contact with nature are perhaps more pertinent in the twenty-first century world of cyberspace and "virtual" realities.

Conclusion

Comstock 5

Works Cited

Heading
centered
First line flush
with left
margin, then
indented

Goodman, Wilson. Orwell's Dark Vision. New York: Columbia UP, 1992.

Janeson, Edward. "Power and Politics in 1984." Modern Fiction Studies.
May 1999: 179–90.

Orwell, George. The Collected Essays, Journalism and Letters of George
Orwell. Ed. Sonia Orwell and Ian Angus. Vol. 4. New York: Harcourt,
1968. 4 vols.

---. 1984. 1949. New York: New Amer. Lib., 1961.

---. The Road to Wigan Pier. New York: Berkley, 1967.

Sandison, Alan. The Last Man in Europe. London: Macmillan, 1974.

Simes, David, ed. British Authors 1900–1950. Oxford: Oxford UP, 1987.

Wolzheck, Nancy. "Orwell Under Fire." Time and Tide. 10 May 2001.
12 Oct. 2003 <http://www.timeandtide.com>.

APA STYLE

Most courses in the social sciences, including anthropology, education, political science, psychology, and sociology, follow the rules for documentation created by the American Psychological Association. For full details,
consult the American Psychological Association's *Publication Manual of the
American Psychological Association*, fifth edition.

STRATEGIES FOR WRITING PARENTHETICAL NOTES

In APA documentation parenthetical notes are placed after material
requiring documentation, and all sources are recorded in a References list at
the end of the paper.

- **Parenthetical notes include author, year of publication, and, for direct quotes, page numbers.** Most sources are identified by the author's
name and the year of publication. Page numbers are usually omitted from
paraphrases but are always included in direct quotations. The information may be placed in a single note or distributed throughout the text:

Smith (2003) suggested that multiple personality disorder was more common than
previously reported.

Continued

It has been suggested that multiple personality disorder is more common than previously believed (Smith, 2003).

Based on recent studies, Smith (2003) asserts that "multiple personality disorder is more common than previously reported" (p. 321).

- **Multiple parenthetical notes indicate more than one source.** If two or more sources are cited within a sentence, notes are inserted after the material quoted or paraphrased:

Johnson (2002) stated that the study "revealed that Chicago schools were adequately staffed" (p. 43), leading Renfro (2003) to reject the teachers' union proposal.

- **For the first text reference, list up to five authors' names:**

Johnson, Hyman, Torque, and Kaiser (2003) observed that computers enhance student performance.

Note: With multiple authors in a parenthetical cite, use an ampersand (&; Johnson, Hyman, Torque, & Kaiser, 2003).

- **For the first reference of a citation with six or more authors, list the first author's name and "et al." (and others):**

Johnson et al. (2003) examined computer education in Chicago, New York, El Paso, and Philadelphia.

- **List corporate and group authors in full initially; then abbreviate:**

Computers are valuable in teaching higher mathematics (Modern Education Council [MEC], 2002). Textbook publishers now include online support for individual tutoring (MEC, 2002).

- **Assign letters (a, b, c) to indicate use of more than one work by an author with same year of publication:**

Kozik (2002a) studied students in Chicago bilingual classes and later reviewed the performance of an English immersion program in San Diego (2002b).

- **Alphabetize multiple sources and separate with a semicolon:**

Several reports suggest that noise pollution can directly contribute to hypertension (Jones, 1997; Smith, 2002).

- **Web sites can be mentioned within the text:**

Chinese educators have attempted to expand Internet access for university students, particularly in the fields of engineering and medicine. Their efforts can be documented by examining Peking University's World Wide Web site at http://www.upkng.eng.edu.

STRATEGIES FOR WRITING
A REFERENCES PAGE

List all the sources you have cited on a separate sheet at the end of your paper titled "References" (center the word References and do not italicize it or place it in quotation marks). If you include works you have read for background but not actually cited, title the page "Bibliography."

- **Arrange the list of works alphabetically by authors' or editors' last names, followed by initials. If no authors are listed, alphabetize by the first significant word of the title:**

  Jones, W. (2002). *Chicago today*. New York: Putnam.
  A new look for Toronto. (2003, Fall). *Toronto Magazine*, 21.

- **For sources with more than one author, alphabetize by the first author's last name and list subsequent authors by last names and initials:**

  Zinter, M., & Ames, J. (2002). *First aid*. New York: Dial.

- **Begin each citation even with the left margin, then indent subsequent lines five spaces. Double-space the entire page. Do not separate entries with additional spaces:**

  Abrams, J. (2002, January 21). Rebuilding America's cities. *Cleveland Plain Dealer*, pp. 1, 7, 8.
  Brown, G. (2003). *The death of the central city: The malling of America*. New York: Macmillan.

- **If more than one source from a given author is used, list the works in chronological order and repeat the author's name:**

  Brown, G. (2003). *The death of the central city: The malling of America*. New York: Macmillan.
  Brown, G. (2000). *Hope for renewal*. New York: Putnam.

GUIDELINES FOR LISTING SOURCES IN REFERENCES AND PARENTHETICAL NOTES

Books

- Write the author's last name, first and subsequent initials:

    Brown, C. W.

- Place the year of publication in parentheses, followed by a period and one space.
- Italicize the full title of the book. Place a colon between the main heading and any subtitle. Capitalize only the first word in the title and any subtitle and any proper nouns or adjectives within the title:

    Brown, C. W. (2003). *Sharks and lambs: Wall Street in the nineties.*

- Record the city of publication and publisher.

    Brown, C. W. (2003). *Sharks and lambs: Wall Street in the nineties.* New York: Kellogg Press.

Note: Do not shorten or abbreviate words like "University" or "Press."

PARENTHETICAL NOTES:

    Brown (2003) stated . . .
    (Brown, 2003)
    (Brown, 2003, pp. 23–25)

Book with Two or Three Authors

REFERENCES ENTRY:

    Smith, D., Johnson, A., & Cook, F. D. (1989). *Writing for television.* New York: Macmillan.

PARENTHETICAL NOTES:

First note:
Smith, Johnson, and Cook (1989) stated . . .

Subsequent notes:
Smith et al. (1989) revealed . . .

First note:
(Smith, Johnson, & Cook, 1989)

Subsequent notes:
(Smith et al., 1989)

Scholarly Article

REFERENCES ENTRY:
Grant, E. (2002). The Hollywood ten: Fighting the blacklist. *California Film Quarterly, 92*, 112–125.
PARENTHETICAL NOTES:
Grant (2002) observes . . .
(Grant, 2002, pp. 121–123)

Newspaper or Magazine Article with Unnamed Author

REFERENCES ENTRY:
The legacy of the Gulf War. (2000, October). *American History, 48*, 23–41.
PARENTHETICAL NOTES:
In "The Legacy of the Gulf War" (2000) . . . ("Legacy," 2000, pp. 22–24)

Note: For parenthetical notes, use shortened titles in quotation marks.

Letter to the Editor

REFERENCES ENTRY:
Roper, J. (1997, June 12). Why the proposed bond won't pass. [Letter to the editor]. *Chicago Defender*, p. B12.
PARENTHETICAL NOTES:
According to Roper (1997) . . .
(Roper, 1997, p. B12)

Other Print Sources

Encyclopedia Article

REFERENCES ENTRY:
Keller, C. (2003). Lisbon. In *Encyclopedia of Europe* (Vol. 8, pp. 232–233). New York: Wiley.
PARENTHETICAL NOTES:
Keller (2003) reports . . .
(Keller, 2003, p. 232)

Encyclopedia Article with Unnamed Author

REFERENCES ENTRY:
Lisbon. (2002). In *Columbia illustrated encyclopedia* (Vol. 10, p. 156). New York: Columbia University Press.
PARENTHETICAL NOTES:
In "Lisbon" (2002) . . .
(Lisbon," 2002, p. 156)

Pamphlet

REFERENCES ENTRY:
Tindall, G. (Ed.). (2002). *Guide to New York churches.* New York: New York Chamber of
  Commerce.
PARENTHETICAL NOTES:
Tindall (2002) noted . . .
(Tindall, 2002, pp. 34–36)

Nonprint Sources

Motion Picture

REFERENCES ENTRY:
Scorsese, M. (Director). (1995). *Casino* [Motion picture]. United States: Universal.
PARENTHETICAL NOTES:
Scorsese (1995) depicts . . .
(Scorsese, 1995)

Television Program

REFERENCES ENTRY:
Hong, J. (Producer). (1997, May 12). *Women at work.* [Television broadcast]. New York: Public
  Broadcasting Service.
PARENTHETICAL NOTES:
According to Hong (1997) . . .
(Hong, 1997)

Videotape

REFERENCES ENTRY:
Freud, J. (Producer), & Johnson, K. (Director). (1996). [Videotape]. *Colonial Williamsburg.* New
  York: American Home Video.
PARENTHETICAL NOTES:
Freud and Johnson (1996) . . .
(Freud & Johnson, 1996)

Speech

REFERENCES ENTRY:
Goode, W. (2003, October 12). *America in the next century.* Address before the Chicago Press Club, Chicago, IL.

PARENTHETICAL NOTES:
According to Goode (2003) . . .
(Goode, 2003)

Electronic Sources

E-mail

Because e-mail is not recorded in archives and not available to other researchers, it is mentioned in the text but not included in the list of references. Treat it as a personal communication—mentioned in the text only, as follows:

PARENTHETICAL NOTE:
Medhin (personal communication, March 1, 2002) suggested . . .
Medhin (personal communication, March 1, 2002)

CD-ROM

REFERENCES ENTRY:
MedNet, Inc. (2002). *Directory of mental disorders* [CD-ROM]. New York: Author.

PARENTHETICAL NOTES:
MedNet (2002) states . . .
(MedNet, 2002)

Electronic Journal

REFERENCES ENTRY:
Smith, P. (2002, March 2). Help for homeless promised. *Psychology Journal.* Retrieved January 25, 2003, from http://www.psychojourn./hts/index

Note: Because the content of websites can change, it is important to list the date you retrieved the information.

PARENTHETICAL NOTES:
According to Smith (2002) . . .
(Smith, 2002)

Article from Online Newspaper

REFERENCES ENTRY:
Gulf war syndrome: Diagnostic survey reveals dangerous trend. (2003, March 11). *New York Times*. Retrieved December 15, 2003, from http://www.nytimes.com/aponline/ap-gulf.html

Note: Do not end the entry with a period if the last item is a URL.

PARENTHETICAL NOTES:
In "Gulf War" (2003) . . .
("Gulf War," 2003)

Database

REFERENCES ENTRY:
Criminal Justice Network. (2002). *Capital cases and defense funding*. Retrieved May 4, 2003, from telnet freenet.crimjus.ca. login as guest, go index (2003, June 23).

PARENTHETICAL NOTES:
According to "Capital Cases" (2002) . . .
("Capital Cases," 2002)

Electronic Texts

REFERENCES ENTRY:
Weston, T. (1989). *The electronic teacher*. Retrieved May 25, 2000, from Columbia University, the Education Server website: http://www.edserv.edu/index.html

PARENTHETICAL NOTES:
Weston (1989) points out . . .
(Weston, 1989)

Web Pages

REFERENCES ENTRY:
Regis, T. (2003, January 5). Developing distance learning. [In *Regis*. Retrieved October 27, 2003, from http://regis.devel/home/distlearng/toc.html

PARENTHETICAL NOTES:
Regis (2003) suggests . . .
(Regis, 2003)

Synchronous Communication

To cite a posting from newsgroups, online forums, and electronic mailing lists, include author's name, post date, message subject line, "Message posted to" followed by the URL.

REFERENCES ENTRY:

> Goring, D. (2003, May 12). Seminar discussion on alcoholism. Message posted to
> Telnet://www.drugabuse.parc. edu:8888

PARENTHETICAL NOTES:

> Goring (2003) indicates . . .
> (Goring, 2003)

FTP

REFERENCES ENTRY:

> Divak, T. (2002). *Cocaine addiction and pregnancy*. Retrieved March 25, 2003, from ftp://
> addiction.sources.com library/article/drugs/c8.txt

PARENTHETICAL NOTES:

> Divak (2002) records . . .
> (Divak, 2002)

Gopher

REFERENCES ENTRY:

> Simes, D. (2003). Understanding Orwell's vision. *English*. Retrieved May 16, 2003, from
> gopher://h-net.ukw.edu/ oo/orwell/internet-cit

PARENTHETICAL NOTES:

> Simes (2003) states . . .
> (Simes, 2003)

SAMPLE RESEARCH PAPER USING APA STYLE
(with Abstract)

Shortened title
and page
number

Heading
centered and
double-spaced

Feeding Frenzy:

Journalism and Justice in

the Leopold and Loeb Case

Sean O'Connell

Criminal Justice 201

May 10, 2004

Abstract

No paragraph
indent

Current popular opinion suggests that recent high profile legal proceedings have been adversely affected by excessive and sensational media coverage. These cases, many argue, have set dangerous precedents which will cause lasting harm to American justice. The 1924 trial of Leopold and Loeb indicates that this is not a new concern. A careful analysis of the role of journalism in what was called "the crime of the century" reveals the media may have undue influence in individual cases but have little lasting influence on the criminal justice system.

Feeding Frenzy 3

Feeding Frenzy:

Journalism and Justice in

Leopold and Loeb Case

Introduction   The twentieth century ended with a flurry of highly publicized crimes and trials—the Menendez case, the O. J. Simpson trial, the Jon Benet Ramsey investigation, and the impeachment of President Clinton. In each instance, the media made instant celebrities of suspects and witnesses. Driven by fame or money, even minor figures became household names, publishing books and appearing on talk shows. Commentators continually lamented that justice was being perverted by media attention, that televised trials were turning lawyers into actors and trials into a kind of theater. Justice, many argued, was being irrevocably damaged.

An earlier case, however, reveals that this phenomenon is not new. In the spring of 1924 two young men committed a crime that made them nationally known celebrities and sparked a firestorm of media attention, which Direct many at the time insisted "damaged justice forever" (Harrison, 1924, p. 8).

Direct
quotation
with author,
year,
page number

The "Crime of the Century"

On May 21, 1924, Jacob Franks, a wealthy Chicago businessman, received news that his fourteen-year-old son had been kidnapped. A letter signed "George Johnson" demanded ten thousand dollars and gave Franks detailed instructions on how to deliver the ransom. Desperate to save his Paraphrase son, Franks complied with the kidnapper's request, but before he could dewith liver the money, he learned his son had been found dead. Less than twelve author and year hours after the abduction, a workman discovered the naked body in a ditch on the outskirts of the city (Arkan, 1997).

The killing of Bobby Franks created a national sensation. Rumors circulated that the kidnapper had been a jealous teacher or a disgruntled employee or customer of one of Jacob Franks' enterprises. Because the body had been stripped, many speculated that the killer had been a sexual pervert (Higdon, 1974).

The press seized upon the story, printing numerous accounts of the police investigation. One paper offered readers a cash prize for submitting the best theory of the case and was swamped with thousands of letters (Higdon, 1974). The police soon had a strong lead. A pair of glasses had been discovered near the body. Though common in appearance, the frames had a newly

Video listed by
title and year

patented hinge. The eyeglasses were quickly traced to a neighbor, nineteen-year-old Nathan Leopold ("Born Killers," 1998).

Nathan Leopold explained he had probably dropped the glasses while leading a birding class a few days earlier. At the time of the crime, he claimed to have been driving with a friend named Richard Loeb and two girls they had picked up in Jackson Park. At first, investigators found Leopold's story believable (Leopold, 1958). Leopold and Loeb seemed unlikely criminals. Like Bobby Franks, they were sons of millionaires; Richard Loeb's father was vice-chairman of Sears & Roebuck. They were gifted students, both having completed college at eighteen. Leopold spoke numerous languages and had become a nationally recognized ornithologist ("Born Killers," 1998). Brought in for questioning, Richard Loeb initially corroborated Leopold's alibi, claiming they spent May 21st with girls they picked up in Jackson Park (Higdon, 1974).

State's Attorney Robert E. Crowe remained unconvinced and continued his investigation. On May 31st, after a long interrogation, Richard Loeb gave a detailed confession, admitting that he and Nathan Leopold were solely responsible for the murder of Bobby Franks. There was no doubt about their guilt. They led police to where they had disposed of the victim's clothing and the lagoon where they had dumped the typewriter used to write the ransom letter (Arkan, 1997). Satisfied he had an airtight case, Richard E. Crowe announced to the press, " I have a hanging case " ("Born Killers," 1998). The stunned Loeb family asked the most famous lawyer of the era, Clarence Darrow, to save their son's life (Leopold, 1958).

The arrest of two wealthy young men, their total lack of remorse, rumors of homosexuality, and the appearance of Clarence Darrow in the case created a media firestorm.

The Chicago Press of the 1920s

At the time of the Franks kidnapping, Chicago had six daily newspapers, including two Hearst publications known for sensational headlines (Higdon, 1974). Newspapers of the era were highly competitive. Attorney and journalism professor David Evans (personal communication, April 2, 2000) notes, "Newspapers in those years were eager to capitalize on crime, sex, and violence to boost sales and increase their advertising rates based on circulation."

Personal
interview,
cited fully in text
but not included
on References
page

Competition led journalists and newspapers to engage in illegal practices. Reporters, whose salaries and bonuses were tied to sales, impersonated police officers to obtain leads, stole documents, and bribed officials for information (Evans, 2000). Major Chicago dailies engaged in brutal circulation wars, hiring gangsters to terrorize newsdealers and newsboys from rival papers. The commuter who stopped at a newstand to purchase a *Herald and Examiner* might be beaten by a thug working for *The Chicago Tribune* (Higdon, 1974; Evans, 2000).

Feeding Frenzy

The Leopold and Loeb case presented the Chicago press with an unparalleled opportunity for sensationalism. For many the case represented the moral degeneration of American youth. The 1920s was an era of youthful rebellion, marked by flappers, speakeasies, and open discussions of sex. Prohibition was widely violated, leading millions of Americans to associate with bootleggers and fuel the growing criminal empires of gangsters like Al Capone (Bergreen, 1994).

The Chicago papers had given great press coverage to the gangland killings of the era. But unlike the crude turf battles of the "beer wars," the Leopold and Loeb case gave reporters new avenues to exploit. They quickly dubbed the case a "Thrill Killing," a crime motivated by something darker and more sinister than simple greed (Evans, 2000). After Leopold and Loeb were arrested, Chicago papers reported extensively on their privileged status and their total lack of remorse. *The Chicago Daily News* referred to the defendants as "jealous actors" who "taunted" each other as reporters watched ("Leopold and Loeb," 1924, p. 4). Stories commented on the stylish dress and demeanor of the two young men, who smoked cigarettes and gave impromptu press conferences. Stating the crime had been an experiment, Nathan Leopold told *The Chicago Daily News*, ". . . it is as easy to justify such a death as it is to justify an entomologist impaling a beetle on a pin" ("Leopold and Loeb," 1924, p. 4).

These stories inflamed the public. Crowds demanded the young men be hanged. Commentators across the country saw the pair as symbols of a corrupt generation without moral consciousness.

The "Trial of the Century"

Despite their confessions, Leopold and Loeb pleaded not guilty. Their attorney, Clarence Darrow, an outspoken opponent of the death penalty, took the case to put capital punishment on trial. Sensing the hostile mood of the jury and cognizant of the crowds milling outside the courthouse demanding the killers be put to death, Darrow changed the plea to guilty (Higdon, 1974).

Darrow's Strategy

Convinced that a jury would not only convict his clients but demand the death penalty, Darrow wanted to avoid a trial. By entering a plea of guilty, Darrow would be able to address the judge directly. He believed he would have a better chance to convince a single individual to spare his clients' lives. A jury, Darrow knew, would make a collective decision. A judge, however, would bear individual responsibility for sending two teenagers to the gallows ("Born Killers," 1998).

Darrow did not consider pleading Leopold and Loeb not guilty by reason of insanity, because this would have required a jury trial. He did, however, argue to Judge Caverly that mental illness should be considered a mitigating factor. He argued that Leopold and Loeb should be imprisoned for life rather than executed (Higdon, 1974).

Press Coverage

The hearing before Judge Caverly became a media circus. Each day thousands of people mobbed the courthouse, hoping to obtain a seat in the courtroom. Admiring women sent flowers to Leopold and Loeb. A despondent man offered to be hanged in their place. A young woman offered to perjure herself, claiming to be one of the girls Leopold and Loeb had picked up in Jackson Park. *The Chicago Tribune,* which owned a radio station, briefly urged readers to demand that the hearing be broadcast over the new medium. Reporters stole a medical report from Darrow's office and printed intimate details about the defendants' sex lives (Higdon, 1974).

When Darrow called psychiatrists to testify on behalf of his clients, William Randolf Hearst offered Sigmund Freud an undisclosed sum to travel to Chicago to comment on the defendants' mental state. Freud declined, but less reputable "experts," including phrenologists, offered opinions to the press. Diagrams of Leopold and Loeb's brains appeared in the paper with arrows pointing to facial features revealing propensities for falsehood and unnatural sexual appetites (Evans, 2000).

Feeding Frenzy 7

Angered by the crime, the public was outraged by the idea that the killers would be let off because they had unhappy childhoods. Widely viewed as spoiled rich kids, Leopold and Loeb received little sympathy in the press. Hundreds of ministers wrote Judge Caverly arguing that they should be put to death. Arguing before the judge, State's Attorney Crowe echoed sentiments expressed in dozens of editorials (Evans, 2000). Having called over a hundred witnesses, Crowe felt confident he had made a compelling case for the death penalty.

Darrow's Use of the Press

Sensing that Judge Caverly would be influenced by community opinion, Darrow sought to defuse some of the negative publicity. Numerous reporters had claimed that Darrow was being paid a million dollars, inflaming public resentment against the affluence of his clients ("Born Killers," 1998; Evans, 2000). Darrow encouraged the fathers of Leopold and Loeb to release a statement to the press asserting that his fee would be determined by the Illinois Bar Association and that their goal was only to secure life imprisonment for their sons. Darrow employed primitive sampling techniques to measure the public mood. He directed pollsters to ask randomly selected men in the Loop if they believed Leopold and Loeb should be executed. Before release of the statement, sixty percent favored the death penalty. After release of the statement, sixty percent agreed that life imprisonment would be a suitable punishment (Higdon, 1974).

According to Evans (2000), the most significant element of Darrow's strategy was an eloquent twelve-hour closing argument against the death penalty. Quoting the Bible, legal scholars, and great works of literature, he delivered a compelling oration. He stressed the youth of the defendants, arguing that in any other case few would see a life sentence for an eighteen-year-old as lenient. After three weeks of deliberating the case, Judge Caverly shocked the press by sentencing Nathan Leopold and Richard Loeb to life plus ninety-nine years. Despite the severity of the sentence, editorials across the country considered the decision a gross injustice. Edna Harrison (1924) wrote a stinging denouncement of Judge Caverly:

Nowhere has justice been more blinded than in this city. It is an outrage that perversion, kidnapping, and murder have been rewarded.

Parenthetical note including two sources

Indented block quotation

The science of psychology reduced crime to an ailment and killers to patients. This case has damaged justice forever. (p. 8)

The Lasting Influence

The fact that the "outrage" occurred in 1924 illustrates the high profile case made no lasting impact on routine criminal investigations and legal proceedings. David Evans (2000) has argued that the case of Leopold and Loeb, like the sensational trials of the 1990s, had no lasting effect on justice:

> Thousands of trials, both fair and unfair, followed the Leopold and Loeb case. In most instances media attention has had little impact on judges and juries. The insanity plea is rarely used and rarely successful. Psychiatric arguments about diminished capacity have become routine but have not significantly altered the rate of convictions or the severity of sentences, which have steadily become longer.

The case of Leopold and Loeb indicates clearly that excessive media coverage may alter the outcome of a particular sensational trial but has no significant influence on the criminal justice system.

REFERENCES

Arkan, J. (1997). *Leopold and Loeb.* Retrieved April 10, 2000, from chicago.crime.com library/article/trials/c15.txt

Bergreen, L. (1994). *Capone: The man and the era.* New York: Touchstone.

Born killers [Television series episode]. (1998). In C. Meindel (producer), *In search of history.* New York: The History Channel.

Harrison, E. (1924) *The case of Leopold and Loeb.* Chicago: Dearborn.

Higdon, H. (1974). *The crime of the century.* New York: Putnam.

Leopold, N. (1958). *Life plus 99 years.* Garden City: Doubleday.

Leopold and Loeb. (1924, June 2). *The Chicago Daily News,* pp. 1–4.

Heading centered

Entries begin flush with left margin

RESEARCH PAPER CHECKLIST

Before submitting your research paper, review these questions:

✔ Does your research paper have a clearly stated thesis?

✔ Do you provide sufficient evidence to support your thesis?

✔ Does the paper focus on your ideas and commentary or does it only summarize other sources?

✔ Do you comment on the quantity and quality of the evidence you have found?

✔ Does the opening introduce the subject, present the thesis, or explain your research method?

✔ Does the conclusion end the paper on a strong point?

✔ Does the paper follow the appropriate style for citing sources?

✔ Questions for your instructor:

- Is my topic acceptable?
- How many sources do I need?
- Does my paper need an outline?
- Which documentation style is required?

E-WRITING: Exploring Research Writing Online

You can use the Internet to understand more about writing research papers.

1. Using a search engine like Alta Vista, Yahoo, or Google enter terms such as "writing research papers" and "evaluating research papers."

2. Use a search engine to locate sites for the Modern Language Association (MLA) and the American Psychological Association (APA). Note their directions for documenting sources.

InfoTrac® College Edition

For additional resources go to InfoTrac College Edition, your online research library, at http://infotrac.thomsonlearning.com

1. Search for articles in technical and academic magazines and note how writers use documentation to support their points of view. How important is documenting sources in persuading readers? Does the appearance of a works cited page or endnotes give a document more authority?

2. Use search terms like "MLA" and "APA" to locate articles about documentation.

A Brief Guide to Documenting Sources

WHAT IS DOCUMENTATION?

Many of the papers you will write in college require documentation—*a systematic method of acknowledging borrowed words and ideas.* Academic disciplines, publications, and professions have specific methods of documenting sources. When assigned a documented paper, make sure you understand the system your instructor expects.

Why Document Sources?

Whatever their discipline or topic, writers document outside sources for three main reasons:

1. *To avoid charges of plagiarism*
   Plagiarism (derived from the Latin word for "kidnapping") refers to stealing or using the words, ideas, or artistic work of others without giving them credit. Some students find it difficult to believe that copying a few paragraphs from *The World Book* or using statistics found on a website can be considered a "crime." But using sources without credit is a theft of intellectual property. Most colleges have strict policies against plagiarism. Instructors routinely fail students who plagiarize papers. Many universities expel students who submit plagiarized assignments. Charges of plagiarism have ruined the careers of famous scholars and diminished the reputation of political figures. Hollywood studios, screenwriters, novelists, rock singers, and rap stars have been sued for stealing ideas, words, or lyrics of other artists. As a writer, you can protect yourself from charges of plagiarism by noting outside sources. *Accurate documentation clearly distinguishes your work from that of others so no one can accuse you of cheating.*

2. *To support a thesis*
   Citing sources not only protects you from charges of cheating but also makes your writing more effective. To convince readers to accept your

thesis, it is important to provide them with evidence. In court, lawyers prove cases by presenting eyewitnesses, expert testimony, and exhibits. As a writer, you can persuade readers to accept your point of view if you provide proof. *The more controversial your thesis, the more readers will demand supporting evidence from credible sources.*

3. *To help readers learn more*
    Your citations not only protect you from plagiarism and strengthen your argument but also show readers where they can obtain additional information, by listing relevant periodicals, books, and websites.

When to Document?

Students are often confused about what they have to document.

What Not to Document

First, you do not have to document all the sources you use. Even if you look up something in an encyclopedia or a website, you do not have to note its use if the information belongs to what researchers call "the realm of common knowledge":

1. *Common expressions or famous quotations*
    You don't need to list the Bible or your edition of Shakespeare if you simply check the wording of a quotation by Jesus or Hamlet. If you refer to statements readers are familiar with, such as Martin Luther King, Jr.'s "I have a dream" or John F. Kennedy's "Ask not what your country can do for you—ask what you can do for your country," you don't have to note their original source. *Less familiar statements, especially controversial ones, must be documented.*

2. *Common facts not subject to change and available in numerous sources*
    You don't have to list the *Encyclopedia Britannica* as a source if you use it to look up where George Washington was born, when *Death of a Salesman* opened on Broadway, when Malcolm X died, or the height of Mount Everest. General facts such as these are not subject to change and are readily available in hundreds of books, almanacs, biographies, textbooks, and Web sites. No one will accuse you of stealing information that is considered standard and widely known by millions of people. *Facts subject to change or dispute, such as the population of Denver, the number of people on death row, or income tax regulations, must be documented.*

What to Document

In almost every other case, you must acknowledge the use of sources:

1. *Direct quotations*
   Whenever you copy word-for-word the spoken or written words of others, you must use quotation marks or block paragraphs to distinguish it from your own text, and you must indicate its source.
2. *Indirect quotations or paraphrases*
   Even if you don't copy information but restate the author's ideas in your own words, you must acknowledge the source. Changing a few words in a quotation or summarizing several pages in a paragraph does not alter the fact that you are making use of ideas and information from another source. Although you don't use quotation marks, you need to indicate that you have borrowed from an outside source.
3. *Specific facts, statistics, and numbers*
   Facts will only be acceptable to readers if they know where they came from. If you state, "Last year eighteen innocent men were sentenced to death for crimes they did not commit," readers will demand the source of this number.
4. *Graphs, charts, photographs, and other visual aids*
   Indicate the source of any visual aid you reproduce in your paper. If you create your own graphics based on statistics, you must indicate where the numbers originated.

Using Quotations

Direct quotations should be used sparingly. Remember, the goal of your paper is to express your own thoughts and opinions, not present a collection of other people's ideas. There are times, however, when direct quotations can be powerful additions to your essay.

Use direct quotations:

1. When presenting a significant statement by an authority or eyewitness.
2. When the statement is unique or memorable.
3. When the idea expresses conflicts with the mainstream of thought or common knowledge.
4. When the original statement is well-written and more compelling than a paraphrase or summary.
5. When readers may doubt a controversial point of view or question that a certain person made the statement.

Direct quotations have to be integrated into the text of an essay in a clear, sensible manner and be documented. (These examples use MLA format; for APA use of quotations, see Using APA Documentation).

1. Indicate short direct quotations (1–4 lines) by placing them in quotation marks followed by a parenthetical citation:

   According to Lester Armstrong, "The university failed to anticipate the impact of state budget cuts" (17).

   Indicate long direct quotations (over 4 lines) by placing them in indented paragraphs without quotation marks. Indent ten spaces on the left side and introduce with a colon:

   According to Lester Armstrong, higher education suffered greatly during the recession:

   > The university failed to anticipate the impact of state budget cuts. As a result, construction on the new stadium was halted. Twenty-five administrators were laid off. Plans to expand the computer labs, bilingual programs, and adult night school were scrapped. The library budget was slashed by 24%, and two daycare centers were closed. The century-old Main Hall, which was scheduled for an extensive refurbishing, was given only cosmetic repairs and painting. (17)

2. Link direct quotations with your text. Avoid isolated quotations:

   Incorrect

   Children are greatly affected by violence on television. "By the time a child graduates from high school, he or she has witnessed over 18,000 homicides on television" (Smith 10). Young people come to view violence, even murder, as reasonable methods of resolving conflicts.

   Blend direct quotations into your text by introducing them:

   Revised

   Children are greatly affected by violence on television. "By the time a child graduates from high school," Jane Smith notes, "he or she has witnessed over 18,000 homicides on television" (10). Young people come to view violence, even murder, as a reasonable method of resolving conflict.

3. You may edit quotations to eliminate redundant or irrelevant material. Indicate deleted words by inserting *ellipsis* (three spaced periods) in square brackets:

Original Text

George Washington, who was heading to New York to confer with his leading advisors, agreed to meet with Franklin in Philadelphia on June 10th.

Edited Quote

As Sanger notes, "George Washington [. . .] agreed to meet with Franklin in Philadelphia on June 10th" (12).

Deletions should only remove unneeded information; they should not alter the meaning of the text by removing qualifications or changing a negative statement into a positive one. It is unethical to alter a quotation, "We should, only if everything else fails, legalize drugs" to read, "We should [. . .] legalize drugs."

4. Insert words or other information to prevent confusion or avoid grammatical errors. For instance, if a direct quote refers to a Frank Bush by his last name and you are concerned readers will confuse him with President Bush, you may insert his first name, even though it does not appear in the original text.

Original Text

Hoping to ease tensions in the Middle East, Bush called for UN peacekeepers to patrol the West Bank.

Quotation

"Hoping to ease tensions in the Middle East, [Frank] Bush," according to *Newsweek*, "called for UN peacekeepers to patrol the West Bank" (14).

If you delete words or phrases, you may have to insert words to prevent a grammar error:

Original Text

Poe and other writers of his generation were influential in shaping a new, truly American literature.

Quotation

According to Sydney Falco, "Poe [. . .] [was] influential in shaping a new, truly American literature" (64).

Using Paraphrases

Paraphrases are indirect quotes. You must document your use of sources, even when you do not copy the text word-for-word. If you read two or three pages of a history book and summarize its points in a single paragraph, document your use of that source. Although you did not directly reproduce any words or sentences, the ideas you present are not your own and should be documented:

Original Text

More than 10,000 of New York's 29,000 manufacturing firms had closed their doors. Nearly one of every three employables in the city had lost his job. An estimated 1,600,000 New Yorkers were receiving some form of public relief. Many of those fortunates who had kept their jobs were "underemployed," a euphemism for the fact that they worked two or three days a week or two weeks a month—or, if they worked full time, were paid a fraction of their former salaries; stenographers, earning $35 to $40 per week in 1928, were averaging $16 in 1933; Woolworth's was paying full-time salesladies $6 per week.

Robert Caro, *The Power Broker* 323–24

Paraphrase

The Depression devastated New York City. A third of the manufacturers shut down operations, and over a million and half New Yorkers were on relief. Those with jobs saw their hours cut and their salaries slashed (Caro 323–24). Conditions in Chicago, Los Angeles, and San Francisco were similar.

Parenthetical references should be placed immediately after the paraphrased material at an appropriate pause or at the end of the sentence.

Using MLA Documentation

The MLA style, developed by the Modern Language Association, is the preferred documentation method used in language and literature courses. In the MLA system, outside sources are listed alphabetically at the end of the paper in a Works Cited list and parenthetical citations are placed after direct quotations and paraphrases. For complete details refer to *The MLA Handbook for Writers of Research Papers*, 6th edition, by Joseph Gibaldi.

Building a Works Cited List

List all sources you refer to under the title *Works Cited* at the end of your paper. Items should be alphabetized by authors' last names or the first significant word of titles if no author is listed.

Sample formats

Book by a single author:
Smith, John. *The City.* New York: Putnam. 2002.
Book by two authors:
Smith, John, and Naomi Wilson. *The New Suburb.* New York: Western. 2001.
   (Only the first author is listed last name, first name.)
Book with more than three authors:
Smith, John, et al. *Urban Housing.* Chicago: Chicago UP, 2000.
   (University Press is abbreviated as UP)
Work in an anthology:
Miller, Arthur. "Death of a Salesman." *American Literature* 1945–2000. Ed. Keisha Sahn
   and Wilson Goodwin. New York: Dial. 2001. 876–952.
Encyclopedia article:
"Miller, Arthur." *The World Book.* 1998 ed.
   (Volume and page numbers are not needed in familiar references)
Periodical article with a single author:
Smith, John. "Urban Planning Today." *American Architect* 25 Oct. 1999: 24–29.
Newspaper article without an author:
"Mideast Crisis Boils Over." *Washington Post* 22 May 2002: A5+.
   (If an article starts on one page, then skips to others, list the first page with a plus sign)
Television program:
"Oil Boom." Narr. Morley Safer. *Sixty Minutes.* CBS. WCBS, New York. 27 Jan. 2002.
   (Include both network and local station with date of broadcast)
Online article:
Wilkins, Robert. "Reflections on Milton." *Michigan Literary Review* 9.2 (1998).
   22 Feb. 2002 <http://www.umichigan.edu/english/litreview.html>.
   (Include both date of access and full electronic address)

Non periodical article on CD-ROM

"Albania." *The Oxford Encyclopedia of Education.* 3rd ed. CD-ROM.
   Oxford: Oxford UP, 2001.

E-mail

Hennessey, Richard. "Re: Urban Planning Conference." E-mail to Sean Brugha. 22 June 2001.
   (Provide name of writer, title of message in quotation marks, recipient, and date)

Intext Citations

As you include direct quotations and paraphrases in your paper, cite their
use with parenthetical notations. These citations should be brief but accurate. If you mention an author or source in your text, you only need to add a
page number:

> Winston Hachner has noted, "The Internet has provided us with a
> dilemma of choice" (874).
>
> *(Note: Place the period after the parenthetical citation)*

If you do not mention the source, include the author's last name or title
with page numbers:

> The Internet has given us more choices than we can process (Hachner
> 874). The sheer volume of information can overwhelm, confuse, and
> strangle businesses accustomed to defined channels of communication
> ("Internet" 34–35).

Sources without page references do not require parenthetical notes if cited
in the text:

> During a Sixty Minutes interview in 2002, Randall Pemberton argued,
> "A terrorist attack in cyberspace can cripple our economy."

You can avoid long, cumbersome parenthetical notes by citing titles or several authors in the text:

> As stated in the Modern Directory of Modern Drama, "August Wilson
> has emerged as one of the nation's most powerful dramatic voices"
> (13). Jacobson and Marley view him as a dominant force in shaping the
> country's perceptions of the African-American experience (145–146).

Using APA Documentation

The APA style, developed by the American Psychological Association, is the preferred documentation method used in social sciences, including psychology, sociology, political science, and history. In the APA style, outside sources are listed alphabetically at the end of the paper in a References list and parenthetical citations are placed after direct quotations and paraphrases. For complete details refer to the *Publication Manual of the American Psychological Association*, 5th edition.

Building a References List

List all sources you refer to under the title *References* at the end of your paper. Items should be alphabetized by authors' last names or the first significant word of titles if no author is listed.

Sample formats

Book by a Single Author:
Smith, J. (2002). *The city.* New York: Putnam Press.
　　(Only authors' last names and initials listed; only first word and proper nouns in title are capitalized)

Book by Two Authors:
Smith, J., & Wilson, N. (2001). *The new suburb.* New York: Western Publishing.
　　(Both authors listed by last name, initial.)

Book with More Than Six Authors:
Smith, J., Wilson, S., Franco, W., Kolman, R., Westin, K., Dempsey, F., Parkinson, J., et al. (2000). *Urban housing.* Chicago: Chicago University Press.

Chapter in an Edited Book:
Miller, A. (2001). Depression in the adolescent male. In J. P. Meyers, J. Reed, & R. Rank (Eds.), *The psychology of youth: Problems and solutions* (pp. 87–99). New York: The Dial Press.
　　(Quotation marks not used in titles of articles and chapters)

Encyclopedia Article:
Depression. (1998). In *The world book* (Vol. 13, pp. 324–325). Chicago: World Book.

Periodical Article with a Single Author:
Smith, J. (1999, October 25). Urban planning today. *American Architect, 63,* 24–29.

Newspaper Article without an Author:
Mideast crisis boils over. (2002, May 22). *The Washington Post,* pp. A5, A8, A14, A26–A27.
　　(If an article starts on one page, then skips to others, list all pages)

Television Program:
Paulus, G. (Executive Producer). (2002, January 27). *The mind* [Television broadcast]. New York: WNET.

Online article:

Wilkins, R. (1998, March). Reflections on depression. *Michigan Science Review, 9,* 116–123.
　　Retrieved October 23, 2001, from http://www.umichigan.edu/science/scireview.html
　　(Include both date of access and full electronic address)

Corporate or organizational Web site without dates:

New York City Health Department. (n.d.). *Bioterrorism.* Retrieved May 12, 2002, from
　　http://www.nychd.org/bioterrorism.html
　　(Cite specific pages where possible rather than home pages)

Article on CD-ROM

Albania. (2001). *Oxford Encyclopedia of Education* (3rd. ed.) [CD-ROM].
　　Oxford: Oxford University Press.

E-mail

E-mail and personal communication are not included in References but are listed within the text by
referring to the writer and date.
　　(R. Hennessey, personal communication, June 22, 2001)

Intext Citations

When you include quotations and paraphrases in your paper, cite their use
with parenthetical notations listing author and year. These citations should
be brief but accurate:

> Hachner (2002) has noted, "The Internet has provided us with a
> dilemma of choice" (p. 12).
> 　　*(Note: Place the period after the parenthetical citation)*
> Wellman (2000) compares two common therapies for treating de-
> pression.
> 　　*(Note: No page references cited for paraphrases)*

For sources without authors, include the first few words of the titles in the
text or a parenthetical citation:

> The *Psychology Year in Review* (2002) presents new theories on ad-
> diction. A recent article reveals a genetic predisposition to narcotic de-
> pendence ("Genetic Maps," 2002).
> 　　*(Include only years even if day and month are available)*

If a work has three, four, or five authors, cite all authors by only last names
in the first reference:

> Bodkin, Lewis, Germaine, and Neimoller (2001) dispute commonly
> held views of addiction.

In subsequent references, cite only the first author:

Bodkin et al. (2001) found no single factor in determining predisposition to alcoholism.

For works with six or more authors, cite only the first author in first and subsequent references:

Bryant et al. (2001) analyzed census figures to determine demographic changes.

STRATEGIES FOR AVOIDING COMMON PROBLEMS

1. *Use outside sources sparingly.* A good essay is not a collection of quotations and paraphrases. The focus of your paper should be your thesis, supporting ideas, and commentary. Avoid using long direct quotations that can be summarized in short paraphrases. *The fact that you find many interesting sources in the library or on the Internet does not mean that you should include everything you find in your paper. Be selective.*

2. *Take careful notes and collect documentation information when you locate valuable sources.*
   Make sure you copy direct quotations carefully word for word and do not distort their meaning by taking ideas out of context. Place direct quotations in quotation marks. If you photocopy a book or periodical, make sure you record the author's name and all publication information needed to document the sources. If you print an article from the Internet, make sure you record the full website address and the date.

3. *Select sources carefully.* Avoid sources that appear biased, outdated, or poorly presented. Remember that all books, periodicals, and Web sites were created by human beings who may be misinformed or prejudiced. Avoid basing your entire paper on a single source. Do not assume that all sources are of equal value. Use critical thinking skills to measure the significance of the sources you locate.

Continued

4. *Comment on the quality and quantity of sources.* Let readers know the results of your research. If sources are limited, outdated, or fragmentary, explain this situation to readers. If you find conflicting evidence or theories, objectively summarize the differences and justify your decisions in selecting sources. Don't assume direct quotations can speak for themselves. Don't insert sources into your essay without commenting on their value and demonstrating how they support your thesis.

5. *Clearly distinguish your ideas from those of others.* Accurate documentation, transitional statements, and paragraph breaks can help readers understand which ideas are solely yours and which ideas originate from outside sources.

6. *Blend quotations and paraphrases into your text to avoid awkward shifts.* There should be smooth transitions between your ideas and those of others.

7. *Be sure to use the documentation system your instructor expects.*